GOLDIE

GOLDIE

Peter Haining

W.H. ALLEN · LONDON
1985

Typeset by Phoenix Photosetting, Chatham
Printed and bound in Great Britain by
Mackays of Chatham Ltd, Kent
for the Publishers W.H. Allen & Co. PLC
44 Hill Street, London W1X 8LB

ISBN 0 491 03144 0

'I think what people like to feel about me is that I'm hopeful, happy and loving. But I'm sure there is somebody out there who is going to say, 'She is full of . . . I don't think that about her at all!'

GOLDIE HAWN
April 1984

Contents

Introduction   9
1 Goldilocks and the Bad Wolves   23
2 Giggle and Peak Time   43
3 America's Favourite Dumb Blonde   57
4 Pure Goldie   77
5 A Journey to Despair   101
6 The Turning-Out Years   123
7 From Private to Superstar   143
8 A Free Spirit   173
Complete Filmography   211
Acknowledgements   216

'Goldie is sexy, funny, beautiful, talented, intelligent, warm and constantly sunny. Other than that she doesn't impress me.' Screenwriter Neil Simon.

Right: 'Eyes like fried eggs
of glee and erotic mischief'
— a cartoon of Goldie by
Gary Smith.

Below: One of the beauties
of Malibu — Goldie
relaxes on the beach near
her home.

Introduction

MALIBU TYPIFIES the American Dream. The azure blue ocean, the dazzling white sands and the rows of opulent beach houses perched along the rolling dunes, bear witness to the life-style and evident wealth of their owners. It has not been called the 'Executive Sandbox' with the densest concentration of personal wealth on earth for nothing.

People in California will tell you that Malibu is famous for being famous: and that consequently it attracts the famous when they become famous. In particular it has become a haven for some of America's best-known film stars and numbers of leading figures in the entertainment business.

It is also, by a curious twist of fate, a notoriously *unsafe* place.

This deceptively beautiful stretch of Pacific coastline is at the constant mercy of high seas, gale-force winds, brush fires, mudslides and even earthquakes. Such indeed was the devastation caused here by a storm in 1979, for example, that the place was actually declared a 'disaster area'.

However, the most insidious danger is surely subsidence. For according to a recent report, the coastline around Malibu is slipping into the ocean at the alarming rate of nearly half an inch a week! It is caused by a geological fault that is gradually eroding away the beach community and some of the million-dollar properties that adorn it.

To certain people this devastating work by Mother Nature seems to rather appositely reflect the risks which threaten the careers of Malibu's celebrity residents: the unexpected element that can cause a slide in popularity into oblivion. And to be sure, the significance of what is happening can hardly be lost on these luminaries even if their careers *do* happen to be on firmer ground than the buildings they own.

The most cynical of those viewing the problems of the com-

9

munity also see it as symbolic of what is happening to the film industry as a whole. Pointing to a drop in standards, a decline in talent, and a general falling-off in film quality. Only television, they grumble, seems to be growing all the time with a kind of relentless mediocrity.

Among the VFS (Very Famous Stars) who have property in Malibu are Cary Grant, Yul Brynner, Paul Newman, Barbra Streisand, Ali McGraw and Goldie Hawn. None is probably likely to be ruined by this freak of nature should it strike their luxury homes.

But nonetheless the gradual subsidence of the houses, as fissures open across the floors and ceilings, and the eerie sound of cracking as the buildings twist and groan under the strain, is a reminder that there *can* be another side to the dream lifestyle that popular belief accords to screen idols.

The plight seems somehow an object lesson in the circumstances that can affect the lives of all men and women – whatever their position in society. And a salutory reminder that no life, however famous it may become, is without its high and low points, its stresses and strains, its times of achievement and of disaster.

From what I have read of the careers of Cary Grant, Yul Brynner, Paul Newman, Barbra Streisand and Ali McGraw, they have all experienced the vagaries of life during their astonishingly successful careers. And from what I have come to learn of Goldie Hawn while investigating her life – and will describe in the pages which follow – this is even truer still . . .

Goldie Hawn is a remarkable person to be sure – as even the most perfunctory glance in any film reference book will quickly show.

Shot to overnight fame on the television show, *Laugh-In* as a giggly 'dumb blonde' who fluffed her lines and hardly filled a bikini, she has since proved herself as a dancer, comedienne, singer and actress (winning an Oscar in the process) as well as a producer, business-woman and movie tycoon who can make Hollywood sit up and take notice. She has been called one of the film city's richest and most successful women. She also happens to be widely loved and respected as well – and has shown herself to be a devoted mother to her two small children.

'I'm a very industrious person ... I have good creative instincts and I can work with business people.' Goldie the producer.

The scrapbook of her career is littered with accolades. Critics have called her 'the hottest comedienne in the movies today' and compared her to Judy Holliday, Marilyn Monroe and the young Bette Davis – while the prestigious American magazine, *Newsweek*, a short while ago made no bones about describing her as 'the most popular actress in America'.

11

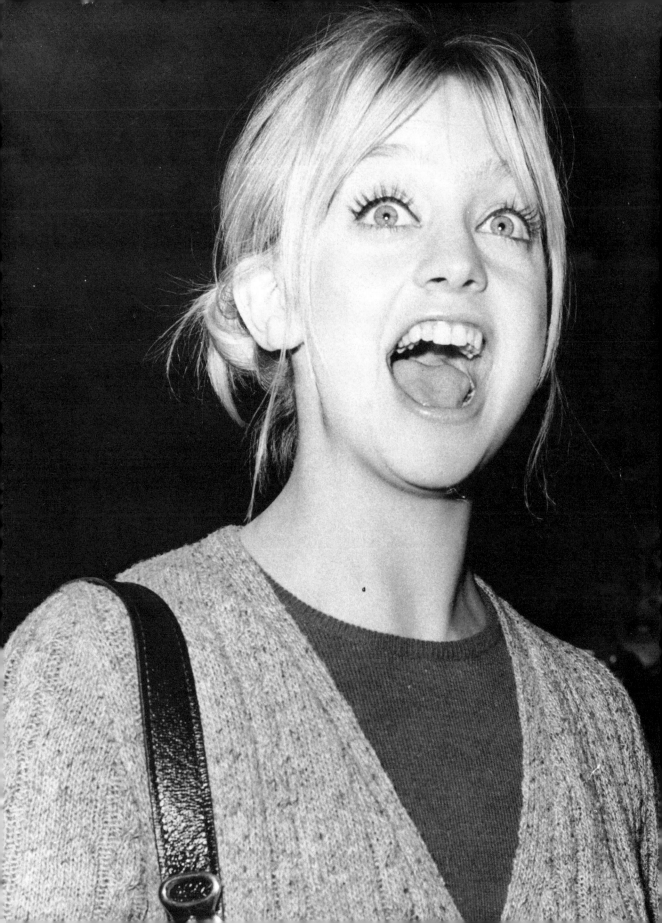

Certainly she is a 'Megabuck Star', to use one of *Variety*'s favourite terms: up there with the Streisands, the Fondas, the Dunaways and the Streeps who can command millions of dollars for their pictures. And certainly, too, she is the latest and most successful in a long line of gorgeous blondes who have won the hearts of cinema audiences everywhere, men as well as women, with the kind of appeal which crosses any barriers of prejudice or sex. She knows why, too. 'Women have never felt threatened by me,' she puts it simply. 'I don't fear people either, and I don't pretend to be something I'm not.'

It's for this reason that the heartaches which have been as much a part of Goldie's life as her success have never been concealed for the sake of any kind of 'image'. (Though Goldie firmly denies she has one.)

'I've had some success acting in movies and producing, and the public seems to like me,' she says with one of those disarming smiles which lights up her whole face. 'But on the other hand, I can't seem to forget that I've had two marriages that went down the drain. I don't suffer daily, but I've paid big prices for my success.'

Hers is indeed a spectacular success which has been earned by all-round show business talent. And though she is now on the verge of forty, there is still something of the child-woman about her. As one admirer said recently, 'As a general rule no one above the age of seventeen should even attempt to be cute – but Goldie Hawn is the perennial exception.'

In person, Goldie is a sparkling, captivating vision of cuddly sex with a direct, calculating way of looking at people that seems to enable her to think her way into their minds. At least that's one man's impression (mine) and it's shared by another, critic David Thomson, who wrote a short while ago, 'Goldie talks so much better and funnier than her films. She is a mixture of the straight-laced and the flirt, of the gamin and the mom, of self-righteous integrity and madcap impulse.'

Her face, as much as anything, has been her fortune. Those saucer-shaped blue eyes – 'like fried eggs of glee and erotic mischief' I once heard them described – and that explosion of straw-coloured hair. The heavy, sensual lips and big, white teeth. The five-foot six-inch tanned figure, lithe, curvy and compact from the days when she was a dancer. Blonde and beautiful she unquestionably is – but dumb? Never!

Goldie during her *Laugh-In* years, photographed in 1969.

Overleaf: Taking time off: a delightful shot of Goldie relaxing with some 'friends'.

'Making it as a dumb, vacant blonde was definitely not the easiest way,' she reflects today, 'although *I* knew I was not that way. It was just so hard to be taken seriously. I recall that the women's movement was sort of beginning then – not that I had anything to do with it. But I really felt I was a kind of misfit, although I was very successful at what I was doing.

13

'Slowly, though, my evolution happened with each film I made. I was very young when I became famous on *Laugh-In*. But luckily I've been able to grow in my strata, both as an actress and as a woman.'

Goldie is, of course, inextricably identified with comedy – and would never want to completely change that – but it is the *kind* of comedy that is important to her. 'I've never been a lover of slapstick comedy,' she says. 'The kind of comedies that attract me have to have substance. They must have a social ramification.'

It is true to say that over the years she has proved herself to be at her best in comedies of character, situation and truth. Yet what comes as a surprise is to learn that she actually doesn't consider herself very funny at all.

'I have never thought I was funny,' she told Miles Harrison in 1982. 'I remember I did a play once, and people were laughing and my mother came back stage and she said, "I don't think you're so funny" and I said, "I don't think I'm so funny, either. I'm the same as I always am." You see, I've never been any different. What I have learned throughout my career in acting is that I know what people respond to about me. It is the idea that I love people, that I love life, that I have a face and a body that are very expressive.

'You can't say that Goldie is just funny because she knows how to deliver a line. It's more than that. It's a whole encompassing, odd little character. This kind of person that *arrived* in the world. For I have *truly* been no different than I was when I was a little child.'

Goldie does accept that she has a gift – and is very grateful for it. 'I have this ability to lift people up and make them laugh. That's not something that's given to everyone and I feel lucky I can do it.'

Despite all the wealth and fame that have come her way, Goldie has never lost this love of life and people. 'Look, I can sit and make conversation with anybody, a road digger or the King of Sweden. Mingling is not a problem for me.'

She likes her privacy, though, and apart from the redwood beach house in Malibu, she has a colonial-style house in Pacific Palisades, a comfortable office in Westwood not far from Hollywood (so she can keep her career and family life separate) as well as retreats in the Northern Californian Sierras and on the Mediterranean island of Ibiza. None, though, have the usual Hollywood ostentatiousness and are furnished with the casual style and good taste of their owner. And although Goldie has household and secretarial staff to enable her to cope with her busy life, she does not see herself as a 'Movie Star' in capital letters.

'I have this ability to lift people up and make them laugh.' Goldie the actress.

17

The three faces of Goldie in her most succesful film, *Private Benjamin* — dumb blonde, comedienne and dramatic actress.

'I don't feel I have that kind of spitfire thing', she explains, 'that mystique that stars are supposed to have. I don't fit into that niche – you know, the Elizabeth Taylor thing. Women like that are always so decked out. They're always *appearing*. I rarely go to functions. I won't own diamonds and furs. I don't perceive of myself as a star. But you have to deal with this fantasy all the time and relate to it.'

Goldie, in fact, is not even one for going to the cinema very often! 'I'm not proud of the fact,' she says, 'but I'm not a film buff. I rarely go to the movies, which is terrible. I do see certain films that I want to see, but I'm not someone who says I've got to see everything that's out. Certainly when it comes to the older films, I love to see them, but I don't go out. I tend to catch them on TV.'

Despite this deliberately selective viewing, she has her favourite movies. 'Two of my very favourites are *Funny Girl* with Barbra Streisand and *Bringing Up Baby* with Katharine Hepburn. I like comedies with appealing female comediennes. I've seen those two films so many times I've lost count. Also, no specific titles but anything with Mae West, except her last two films.'

It would be quite wrong, however, to imagine on such evidence that Goldie is anything other than totally dedicated to her art. 'I'm a very industrious person,' she says. I'm always thinking about what I'm going to do every moment. If I'm not doing a film, then I'll learn a language or something.'

And she has brought the same dedication to her recent work as a producer. 'I don't actually think of myself as a business-woman,' she told a group of journalists after making *Private Benjamin* in 1980. 'I mean, maths was not my best subject at school. But I have good creative instincts and I can work with business people. I'm also a diplomat. Yes, a good word for me is industrious.'

Goldie has also been unceasingly conscientious and loving in raising her two children, Oliver and Kate, since her divorce from their father, Bill Hudson, who was her second husband. This combination of motherhood with a super-successful career has made her a model for many women and an object-lesson for perhaps even more.

'My children and my home life are very important to me,' she says, 'but I'm not forfeiting my life, my career, the things that I do. I'm combining them and finding that you *can* do that.'

Both the men and the women who know Goldie have nothing but praise for her. Typical of the warmth shown towards her is that given by the veteran screenwriter, Neil Simon, who wrote one of her most successful pictures, *Seems*

Like Old Times, and quipped in 1980, 'She's sexy, funny, beautiful, talented, intelligent, warm and constantly sunny. Other than that, she doesn't impress me.' And film critic Barbara Paskin who has frequently interviewed her says that to attack Goldie 'would be like kicking a kitten'.

Goldie acknowledges the debt she owes to her parents for her success: the support and encouragement of her mother through all the ups and downs, and the warmth and good humour of her father. Ed Hawn, she says, gave her the best piece of advice she ever had. He told her, 'Goldie, you're an extraordinary woman who lives an extraordinary life. Stop trying to apply the norm to yourself because your life will never be everyone else's definition of normal.'

In looking back over the four decades of her life, Goldie can see the wisdom of her father's words, and adds reflectively: 'I've always been a very optimistic person. Whether I have talent or not isn't the real issue. For whatever reason, I'm one of the chosen ones who was able to get the breaks and become successful. And I always say that no one can judge themselves by me, because I'm a fluke. People have to judge themselves by what *they* are doing.'

But surely the very fact that she can call herself a fluke underlines the reason why there is such public interest in her extraordinary success story? And the interest is only made more intriguing when she grows really serious and makes remarks such as this:

'People have never wanted to see, still less accept, the darker side of Goldie Hawn. They see only the light comedienne. But I have been through some terrible times in my life. Like most people I have undergone pain and disappointment. But I have also had my dreams shattered and two marriages wrecked by money and success.'

The story of Goldie's life, in fact, is neither solely one of despair and heartache or one of triumph and acclaim. But rather a rich mixture of all these elements resulting in a unique lady with a very special talent.

'For whatever reason, I'm one of the chosen ones who was able to get the breaks and become successful.' Goldie the super-star — with Burt Reynolds.

1 Goldilocks and the Bad Wolves

THE PLACE is New Jersey, around midnight. Across the distant black expanse of the Hudson River, the lights of New York – Manhattan in particular – glisten and sparkle in the late summer air. To the teenage girl hurrying down the block they look almost fairy-like – and, despite the heat, are somehow a reminder of home and the colour and gaiety of childhood Christmases years ago.

But the blonde-haired, rather waif-like girl with saucer-shaped blue eyes has no time for thoughts of the past. There are rather more pressing matters on her mind. Like the twenty-five very necessary dollars she is going to earn from go-go dancing in a night club somewhere on this block.

For a girl who has her sights on stardom – even a modest stardom – the booking at what she knows instinctively is going to prove yet another sleazy dive inspires little confidence or enthusiasm. But living in New York, even as far from the bustle and glamour of Manhattan as Eighth Avenue, still costs money, although you share a tiny apartment with four other young girls. So she plucks up her courage, at last finds the dingy entrance to the nightclub, and goes in . . .

Years later, when her circumstances are very different, that same girl recalls the night as clearly as if it were yesterday. Not that many people would be likely to forget – or perhaps have to endure – such an experience in their early days as an entertainer.

'I was booked at this after-hours place in New Jersey,' the girl says. 'I had just enough money to take a bus. When I got there, I found it was the worst bar you could imagine – dark, sleazy, dirty. It had one barmaid, and right off the bat the owner, who was drunk, tried to make me.

'There were four customers sitting out front and when they saw me, they began to chant, "Make her dance! Make her

'Goldilocks' — the bubbly blonde on her way to stardom.

23

Goldie's father, Ed, appearing with her in Las Vegas.

dance!" So I climbed up on this wobbly table. Someone put a dime in the jukebox – that was the kind of joint it was – and I began to dance. And then it happened.

'One of the customers, sitting a few yards in front of me, unzipped his zipper. And he began to expose himself. I kept looking away. The other guys were howling. I was in a den of perverts!

'I thought I was going to blow my mind. I danced faster and faster. I was supposed to get twenty-five dollars for the night. "To hell with it," I said finally. I was so frightened I ran out of the place. I didn't even have money for a bus fare. So I hitched a ride with a truck driver back to the city. It was a nightmare from start to finish.'

Goldie Hawn was still a few months short of her nineteenth birthday when she fled from that New Jersey dive. And although she had been in some similar places before – and would find herself in some pretty uncomfortable spots again –

Goldie with her mother,
Laura, at a press conference.

it was an understandably horrifying experience for a young girl from a sheltered, middle-class American background. It was, though, to play a part in helping develop the tough and resilient side to her character which would later prove so important in her rise to stardom.

Indeed, life in New York in 1964 when star-struck Goldie first arrived proved anything but the giggle her famous personality might have you believe. She was an unknown, and life was an unrelenting grind both working (whenever she could find it) and getting by in a hostile environment that had already broken the heart and spirit of many a hopeful youngster like herself.

Driven by the desire to become a successful dancer, Goldie had come to New York at eighteen because, as she said, she felt if she didn't make her move then she would soon be too old. For the 'Big Apple' was where the action was – clubs and shows just crying out for dancers. Or so she thought.

25

Goldie was fortunate in finding a tiny, one bedroom apartment to share with a group of girls like herself. But the neighbourhood of Eighth Avenue gave her the horrors: it was a haven for prostitutes and drug addicts. To distract herself she endlessly scoured the pages of the newspapers and show business publications like *Variety* looking for jobs. And she blotted out her misgivings by fantasising over the audition announcements.

'I'd just sit there and imagine that every part was perfect for me,' she recalls. 'It was all fantasy, of course, because I didn't have the ambition to go out and audition. Instead I collected unemployment cheques and found what work I could as a go-go dancer.'

The first booking of any importance Goldie remembers was at the giant World's Fair complex in the heart of Queens on Flushing Bay. It had just opened in 1964. She travelled up each day on the subway and appeared in the Texas Pavilion. Curiously, her role in the chorus, ostensibly celebrating the beauties of the great western state, was to perform the famous French dance, the Can-Can! In hindsight, it might seem that the element of comedy which was to be the hall-mark of her success entered her professional career at a very early date indeed!

After the comparative sophistication of the World's Fair, there came a host of short-lived engagements in New York clubs and discos. The bookings were often only for a single night, sometimes paid as little as ten dollars, and usually meant she danced on a pedestal, or a table, or even in a cage slung up above the heads of leering, generally drunken customers! Night after night for hour after hour Goldie twisted and gyrated her slim body which, she remembers, was usually suffering from the lack of a substantial meal.

'Often when I was dancing in those cages with men's noses pressed up against them, I used to ask myself whether it was really worth it,' she says today. 'It was certainly a one-way ticket to aching bones.' Then she gives a little smile and adds: 'My motor was always running then. And, boy, do you get shook up doing that for hours on end!'

These engagements were usually at night, so plucking up her courage Goldie at last began to try out for parts on the stage. She turned up for Broadway shows and night club entertainments. She even auditioned for a job as one of the Copacabana girls at the much-vaunted New York night spot — but was told she 'wasn't sexy enough'.

Years later she was to recall, 'I never made Broadway, although I tried a lot. I would go out to see what was on offer, but you know sometimes it was no better than what I had.

There seemed to be more colour and excitement in what I was already doing!'

Though no one denied her vigour and athleticism as a dancer, Goldie's thin body and flat chest was a world away from the voluptuous girls the showmen were looking for. Even so, she got her fair share of propositions from men.

'Those dance auditions were awful,' she says. 'You'd find these guys just hanging around trying to pick up women for other things. I had some pretty bad experiences during my dog days.

'But they were not all bad because I got over them *and* I learned about the world of show business from the bottom up. I came face to face with some of the dregs of society and also realised what it was like to have both men and women regarding me purely as a sexual creature, you know, coming on to me, propositioning me.'

From those 'dog days' – the term she coined for her period of struggle in New York – Goldie particularly remembers a well-known cartoonist who enveigled her into his plush Park Avenue apartment. She had been naive enough to believe his story that he had seen her dancing and wanted to help her in her career. He said he wanted her to audition for a part in a film he said was going to be based on his comic strip. The film soon proved to be non-existent, and the strip he had in mind was anything but comic.

When Goldie reached the man's apartment she found him clad only in a dressing gown. For a while she went along with his request to lift her skirt so he could sketch her legs. Then he asked her to come closer and she found herself undergoing a rather more sophisticated reprise of the experience in the New Jersey night club. The man pulled back his dressing gown and exposed himself.

Goldie was at first horrified – then just as quickly blazing with rage. 'No way am I going to do *that* to further my career!' she shouted at the man as she stormed out of the flat.

'Then, my dear,' the man sneered after her as he pulled his dressing gown together again, 'I suggest you go back home and marry a nice Jewish dentist!'

Still flushed and angry, Goldie did not stop to think until she was once again back in Park Avenue and heading towards the pokey little apartment in Eighth Avenue she called home. And when she did begin to think of just how little she had achieved since she had left home, she began to wonder if it *had* been such a good idea to turn her back on everything that had been part of her life for the past twenty years . . .

Overleaf: Music-lover Goldie lost in a world of her own.

Takoma Park in Maryland is one of those pleasant suburbs of

27

Washington DC that exudes the style and confidence of people living in the proximity of the capital city of America. Well planned, well preserved and quite obviously affluent, it exemplifies Middle America. Although a few of its citizens commute to jobs with the government in Washington, more are drawn to the spread of local industries around the town.

Edward Rutledge Hawn who lived with his wife, Laura, in a Tudor-style house at the end of a cul-de-sac in Takoma Park, had a tenuous connection with government, although his day-to-day job at the end of the Second World War was running a watch repair store. This, though, was not his main interest – that was music, and in particular the violin, although he was also skilled on the clarinet and saxophone. He had toured as a semi-professional musician before the war, and was later to achieve his ambition of becoming a full-time professional.

Born in Arkansas of Presbyterian stock, Ed Hawn was a direct descendant of John Rutledge of South Carolina, the youngest signatory of the Declaration of Independence in 1776, and later to become the Governor of his home state. Ed had met Laura Speinhoff, an attractive Jewish girl in the 1930s and together they set up home and business in Takoma Park where in 1937, their first daughter, Patty, was born. The war which soon after followed and interrupted the lives of many American families, also put a stop to the Hawns having any more children until 1945.

And then on November 21, Laura Hawn gave birth to a second girl, a lively, elfin-faced infant who was named Goldie Jeanne Hawn.

In the early years of her childhood, Goldie was to hate her first name because along with her mass of curly blonde hair it earned her the nickname from other children of 'Goldilocks'. One day, after some particularly spiteful teasing, she fled in tears to her mother and demanded to know why she had been given such a 'silly name' as it always seemed to be getting her into trouble.

'Because,' her mother answered gently, taking the crying child into her arms, 'you were named after an aunt who everyone thought was the kindest, nicest, most generous women who ever lived.'

And as Goldie dried her tears, her mother added: 'And who will ever forget a name like that?'

A great many years later when she was world-famous, Goldie had to admit that her mother had been absolutely right!

The world of music and in turn entertainment intruded into the child's life almost at once, for Ed Hawn was forever practising his violin or other instruments, and frequently invited fellow musicians into his home. Mrs Laura Hawn recalls,

From her childhood
Goldie loved dancing —
and through it she took
her first steps to fame.

'Goldie grew up in an environment of music and dance. She responded to it from a very early age. I remember at the age of three she climbed up onto the stool of our piano and tried to play. The first thing she did learn was "Happy Birthday". I guess you could say *that* was her debut as an entertainer!'

The atmosphere of the Hawn household was always alive with laughter and good humour, and Goldie had an idyllic childhood as she has always been quick to admit.

'I know it sounds corny,' she says, 'but I had an absolutely *lovely* childhood. I was pretty imaginative, though, and the only bad spot I can remember was this dream I used to have about a woman who lived down the street. In the dream she was always ugly and looked like a witch and was threatening to get me!'

Another childhood memory she talked about years later was of running naked through a backyard portraying a cherub! But whether this was a piece of fantasising or another dream she has never made clear!

Goldie's father was unquestionably a big influence on the development of her sense of humour. 'My Dad had this great sense of fun,' she has recalled, 'and he taught us always to laugh at ourselves. I remember he played at all the Presidential inaugurations, and at weddings and embassy parties in Washington. There would be all sorts of people there from Roosevelt to King Farouk of Egypt and he'd come home with funny, sarcastic things to say. He was the first person to get a giggle out of me and I guess that's where I got my sense of humour from.'

Of her mother, Goldie says, 'She was a pragmatic, strong, extremely self-disciplined woman. You could never call her an ordinary housewife. She and my Dad raised me with a mixture of love and discipline and gave me every opportunity to develop whatever talents I might have had. You certainly couldn't say I went into the entertainment business because of a need to be loved.'

Because Laura Hawn had been a dancer when she herself was young, it was no surprise that she should encourage Goldie to take this up, and when she was three, the tiny, lithe little girl was enrolled as the youngest pupil at the Roberta Fera School of Dance in Takoma Park.

'I think my mum saw me as another Ginger Rogers,' Goldie smiles at the recollection, 'but my idols were to become women like Ingrid Bergman [with whom, of course, she was to appear in her first major film, *Cactus Flower*] and Bette Davis.'

A career in show business was far from her thoughts in her young days, however. For as she revealed only a short while ago, her childhood dream was to be a secretary! 'I always

Haunted by memories — Goldie in a moment from one of her later films, *Foul Play*.

32

wanted to shuffle papers around,' she said, 'I'd sit at a desk at home with a typewriter and an imaginary intercom. Then I'd press it and say, "Yes, Mr Smith, I'll be right in," and take my pencil and pad and go through the door into the next room. That lasted until I was eight!'

Even if she didn't yet see herself as an entertainer, Goldie was still an enthusiastic and hard-working pupil at the dance school, and proved to have a natural ability for classical dancing. It was ballet, though, that particularly took her fancy, and she soon had her heart set on being a ballerina. However, her parents were also encouraging her to spread her interests widely by studying the piano and taking up acting.

'My mother wasn't a stage mother or anything like that,' Goldie insists, 'It was just that she said she had recognised something in me even when I was a baby. She felt there was something about me that was magnetic and it ought to be cultivated. She also used to say, "If you learn to dance, Goldie, it will open doors for you!"'

Apart from the formal work at the Roberta Fera School, Goldie also got into the habit of giving impromptu performances at home, and soon show business began to look a lot more attractive than the life of a secretary. 'I suppose it was inevitable,' she says today. 'And I guess I got a head start by being born into such a colourful family.'

Her first actual public performance occurred when she was eight years old and in the third grade at Takoma Park Junior High School. She had decided to dance to the music of her favourite record 'Sleighride' in the annual talent show. And because a streak of determination was already very much part of her character, Goldie practised her routine for weeks beforehand.

But with a day to go before the performance, disaster struck. Taking the brittle old 78 rpm record off the turntable of the record player she laid it down for a moment on a chair – and then absentmindedly sat on it!

Goldie was distraught, and all the next day Mrs Hawn scoured the local record shops for a copy of the disc. Fortunately, she was able to find one, and Goldie made her appearance: though not without some misgivings because she was *still* convinced her routine was not quite right!

Two years later, when she was ten, Goldie's prowess as a ballerina had progressed to such a point that when a group of girls from the Roberta Fera School were invited to participate in a performance of The Nutcracker Suite being staged by a visiting ballet company, she was among the lucky ones selected to appear. Goldie still remembers the excitement she felt dancing the part of Clara in that presentation by the Ballet

'I had some pretty bad experiences during my dog days.' There were plenty of hard times for Goldie on her way to the top.

34

Russe de Monte Carlo – and indeed still has the cheque for fifty dollars, which she received, framed on the wall of her office in Westwood!

Because her father was often playing his clarinet and saxophone in the house, Goldie developed a passion for dancing to popular music – especially modern jazz – and by eleven she had also become an accomplished tap dancer. The idea of being a ballerina was now fading in her scheme of things.

She suspected, though, that her scatty sense of humour, her occasional bouts of silliness and perhaps most of all her infectious giggle, might make it difficult to convince people that she *could* be serious whenever she chose to be.

'I've always been a giggler,' she smiles. 'Right from being a toddler, my parents used to go along with my silliness with very good humour. It was amazing that they could tolerate me at times!'

Nonetheless, Goldie decided to have a serious try at acting when she entered Montgomery Blair High School. She threw herself enthusiastically into the annual shows and senior plays and also joined 'The Powder Puffs', a group of girls who did all the make-up for the school productions.

Goldie admits there was also another ulterior motive for this frenzy of activity. She was hoping to become popular with boys!

Though now widely considered to be one of the most attractive women in show business, Goldie Hawn was a skinny and very self-conscious young girl in her early teens.

'I didn't feel I was all that pretty as a kid,' she says. 'When I was thirteen I wasn't very well developed physically. In fact I was very, very flat-chested. So I used to feel terribly inferior whenever I saw beautiful girls. Consequently, mine was a more difficult adolescence than most girls have.

'I'd cry sometimes and run home to Mom and ask, "When am I going to be a wow like other girls?" Mom always used to reply, "Don't worry, Goldie, you have something else – personality. One of these days you won't be able to control all those boys who are going to come around." And I'd say, "Oh?" and start bawling again!'

Despite her mother's assurances that she had a lot to offer, Goldie still couldn't seem to attract the boys. She was always the wallflower at the dances and the girl who was never asked for a date. So in desperation she took to wearing falsies and flared petticoats to give her more of a figure, and lashings of make-up to make her – so she thought – more beautiful. She even took to playing practical jokes to get herself noticed.

But her teachers knew this was not the real Goldie – and so did she. 'I had to learn to bring out that special quality my

Mom talked about and develop it,' she said. 'All of us have it, beautiful, plain or ugly, but only a fraction of us realise it fully. Finding it and utilising it is part of discovering your identity.'

It was as she turned sixteen that Goldie really began to appreciate that it was her bubbly personality and ability to dance – her natural attributes not those artificial ones she tried to put on – that would attract people to her, male as well as female.

'I wasn't properly aware of whatever talent I had while I was at school,' Goldie now admits. 'I just discovered it as time went on, doing different parts and hearing laughs from the audience when I didn't expect them.'

Richard Pioli who was Goldie's drama teacher at Montgomery Blair High School remembers her days with him very well. 'She had an innate talent for performing,' he says, 'and she was smart as a fox. Dance was always her first love, she was a natural performer – fluid and able to make it look like she was having a great time on stage.'

Goldie's first role in a school production was as a member of the chorus in a lively version of the musical *Carousel*. That passed by almost unnoticed – but not her appearance in the following year's musical, *Bye, Bye Birdie*. She played Mrs Knox, the wife of the Mayor of Sweet Apple who is almost seduced by the singing heart-throb, Conrad Birdie. And at one point in the play as she was avoiding the singer's advances, Goldie inadvertently tripped over a piece of scenery creating a moment that was pure Chaplin. It was just the kind of scene she was to play years later with such hilarious effect in *Laugh-In*.

As Goldie became more involved with acting, she discussed her future with Richard Pioli. 'We had long talks,' he remembers. 'She expected she would go on to be a dancer. She really only got interested in the theatre after High School. Her parents gave her a tremendous amount of support, though.'

Goldie in fact put her interest in dancing into a still more positive form during the last years at school by opening her own dancing school in the summer months. It was a bold move for the young girl, but it revealed a growing confidence in her own ability. For not only had she to manage the business side of 'Goldie's School of Dance' but she also had to instruct girls who in some instances were as old as she was. But such was the captivating way in which she taught that the classes were always packed and she rarely had a discipline problem.

'I loved teaching,' she says with a nostalgic smile, 'and I always said if I didn't make it in show business I'd teach for the rest of my life. Indeed, I might even go back to it one day.'

But even with the commitment of the classes, Goldie could not resist the challenge of the theatre and would occasionally try for a part with local repertory groups. In 1962 she won a small part in the Virginia State Company's production of a passion play called *The Common Glory* which was staged in Williamsburg, Virginia. That appearance marked her first real public debut.

'It was terrifying,' is all she can remember, 'but somehow magical.'

Not long afterwards, Goldie learned that the Company was putting together a touring company for a summer-long run of Shakespeare's classic, *Romeo and Juliet*. Here was a real challenge, she thought. But she decided she didn't want a supporting role – only the lead would do. So before the audition she memorised the entire part of Juliet.

The competition was stiff, but Goldie sensed she was facing a crucial moment in her life. She was *determined* to get the part – and get it she did. By all accounts her performance as the tragic heroine was outstanding and it proved to Goldie that she could be a serious actress if she chose.

'That was one of the great moments of my life,' she recalls, her eyes sparkling with the memory. 'The first time I realised I could act. I was just eighteen when I did *Romeo and Juliet*. There were 3,000 people in this open-air theatre, and I was just into Juliet's potion speech – "I have a faint cold fear thrills through my veins" – when it suddenly started to rain.

'For a moment I didn't know what to do, then I realised no one had moved. I carried on and the rain got heavier. I saw that I was holding the audience with my acting and so I went on. Still no one moved despite the fact they were all getting drenched. At the end people were actually crying in the rain!

'I was so up after the performance that I had to play classical music to get myself down. Lots of violins – I love violins. They make me cry. It really was the most fantastic experience and from that moment on I felt a little security in myself. At last I knew that I had it in me.'

But it was soon back to earth for Goldie in the autumn of 1963 when she began working for her college degree at the American University in Washington DC. Although she proved to be only a moderate student where scholastic work was concerned, she came alive in her drama classes. She made a considerable impact on her teachers, one of whom is reported to have told her: 'You're good. Why are you still at University? You should be in Hollywood!'

Apocryphal or not, this story mirrored what was going on in Goldie's mind. She couldn't somehow see herself finishing the

Although an attempt to be
a model failed, Goldie maintained her sense of humour
through everything...

four-year course she was embarked upon. But leave Washington? Go 3,000 miles west to Hollywood? And what could she hope to find there for her? At eighteen, her experience was still very limited – and Goldie knew she wasn't exactly the kind of voluptuous, sexy blonde who would instantly capture a producer's eye.

So she turned for advice to the people she trusted most – her parents and her former drama coach, Richard Pioli. Her teacher was in no doubt. 'I have great faith in your ability,' he told her. 'Believe in yourself. You *can* be a star.'

Though Goldie's mother and father had the natural reservations any parents might have at the thought of their teenage daughter leaving home, they both believed that what lay ahead was somehow predestined. 'If you feel dropping out of college and trying to be an entertainer is right for you,' Ed Hawn told her, 'then that is what you must do.' But what neither he or his wife knew was *where* she should go. It was Goldie herself, in fact, who decided that New York was perhaps a rather less ambitious show business citadel for a dancer to storm than the daunting film capital.

'There was never any conflict or opposition to my decision,' says Goldie looking back. 'My parents didn't object. They knew I was vulnerable, but that I was strong also. Like my mother.'

Years after these events, Laura Hawn was to remark, 'I knew she had a talent. And I knew that show business would find her. Would I have allowed her to go to New York when she was only eighteen if I did not?'

The evidence is plain that she would not. But Mrs Hawn could have had little idea of the dramas that were to face young Goldie in New York before that elusive success found her . . .

2 Giggle and Peak Time

THOUGH GOLDIE Hawn's entry into the world of entertainment in New York was via the raw end of the business, it nonetheless sharpened her resolve, built up her physical and moral strength, and also enabled her to learn all about the demands of performing in the tough 'school' of seedy night clubs and after-hours dives. Though go-go dancing was a long way from the classical ballet that had first started her on her way towards being an entertainer, it had its rewards.

'Being a dancer like that you really get to see where it's at and what you're worth,' she says, 'if you can take being treated like a piece of trash and survive you'll come through in the end.'

Goldie's determination was strengthened by the influence that had made her what she was. She explains, 'All my childhood memories were pleasant. There was no conflict, no push and no competition in my family. So when I decided to go into show business no one disagreed. My father believed we should do what we wanted.'

It was the inner strength and peace of mind those feelings gave her, Goldie is convinced, that enabled her to take what followed. The back-breaking hours of dancing, the loneliness and sometimes hunger, and even the coarse propositioning by men who saw her as a typical dumb blonde from the sticks who would make an easy lay.

'That was the worst, the dregs,' she recalls. 'I had more than my share of guys giving me a rough time – being pinched by every guy who thought I was another blonde pushover.

'I never danced topless, though. For one thing, I didn't have enough equipment. But I did have a flimsy little outfit I made myself covered with sequins. And I danced in cages, on pedestals, on tables that wobbled – in the worst dives you can imagine.'

The face that launched a million laughs! Goldie in her television days.

43

At one point, desperate for something a little better, Goldie even tried modelling. The memory still makes her shudder.

'Once when the things were really going badly in New York I tried to be a model,' she says. 'I found an agency willing to take me – the only one to be honest with you – and they shot me off to a photographer. He invited me into his dark room to watch him develop the pictures. But no sooner had we got in there than he leaped on me, hands everywhere. So I gave up the idea of modelling!'

Her plight deepened in 1965 when she was involved in a car crash which almost cost her her life. 'The doctor at the hospital told me it was a miracle I survived,' she remembers. The crash understandably left her nervous of cars, and to this day she prefers to drive herself rather than be a passenger.

But Goldie would not give in – and gradually her determination led to better engagements. Not much better – but at least an improvement on dives like the club in New Jersey. She began to get bookings in the city, and then an engagement at a fashionable new Manhattan discotheque called 'Dudes 'n Dolls'. There were some small roles singing and dancing in off-Broadway productions and even a three-month contract that took her out of the city to San Juan. Here she joined the chorus in a revue being staged at a luxury hotel.

Once again, though, the sheer monotony of the work as well as the poor pay caused Goldie to quit and return to New York – though she was at least two hundred dollars better off than when she had left. This carefully saved money *could* have given her security for a few weeks, but Goldie splashed almost all of it on a little dog she named 'Lambchop'.

She still thinks of this little pet with great affection. 'I was very close to him,' she told an interviewer in 1976. 'He was my best friend. He was a little brown poodle. I never groomed him or anything. He was a mess. But he had great spirit and went everywhere with me.'

'Lambchop' was to prove the first of a string of animals that pet-lover Goldie has surrounded herself with to this day.

Down to her last twenty-five dollars and with no work in sight, Goldie was facing yet another crisis when right out of the blue came a telephone call from the other side of America. At a stroke it changed everything.

The call was from a friend who was working as a choreographer in California. Quit New York, the girl urged her, come to the Golden State.

'She said there was work there which would suit me,' Goldie recalls. 'I didn't give it a second thought. I left everything – except my dog – and just headed west. I never went back.'

The warm, sunny climate of California soon restored her

'This girl certainly had something — she didn't look like the usual stereotyped chorus girl.' Goldie's manager, Art Simon.

45

complexion which was grey from too many late nights in smokey night clubs, and her skin took on the honey brown complexion that heightens her attractiveness. New York soon became little more than a bad dream.

The job her choreographer friend had in mind was at the Melodyland Theatre in Anaheim not far from Hollywood. The engagement was for a whole season and apart from giving Goldie the opportunity to express herself more fully as a dancer, also gave her some valuable lessons in the art of choreography. There was the added excitement of being close to Hollywood, too.

Next came some slightly bigger parts singing and dancing in revivals of two popular stage musicals, *Kiss Me Kate* and *Guys and Dolls* being taken on tour as 'tent shows'. Though these travelling productions were again very demanding in terms of time and energy, they added to Goldie's ever-expanding knowledge of the world of entertainment. She was also greatly encouraged by a comment made unexpectedly by her friend:

'Goldie, I have this feeling something very big is waiting for you here.'

These were the first words of unsolicited praise she could remember since leaving home.

The 'something big' didn't materialise right away, however. After the engagement with the tent shows finished, she accepted a booking in Las Vegas at the prestigious Desert Inn. She knew it would be hard in the timeless world of Vegas where the spinning of the roulette wheels rather than clocks marks the passing of the hours – but she hadn't quite expected to find herself dancing from 10 pm to 5 am! There was the compensation of more varied dancing than usual – including several jazz-inspired routines – but once again she found herself on an entertainment conveyor belt.

Goldie the animal-lover — with one not-so-average pet!

There was, though, the momentary distraction of making a television commercial which brought her into contact with the world of filming for the first time. She was approached by a representative of a TV Commercial casting agency to play a small part in an advertisement for a hair spray. Great, thought Goldie – until she found she had to wear a red wig over her golden locks! And any thoughts this might be a break for her, a step up the ladder, were cruelly shattered as soon as she saw the finished commercial.

'There I was on the screen in this red wig,' she says with a shudder. 'God, I was ugly! I took one look and said, "There's no way I'm going to make it in Hollywood like that!" Although all I really wanted to do was dance, I figured I might just make it on TV. But even without the wig I thought I still didn't look good enough.

'So I decided to get a club act together – me and two guys I had met. I said, "I'll sing and you guys will play and we'll travel around." First, though, I called my Dad. I said, "Daddy, I've made a decision. I want to go on the road and work the clubs."

'Now he'd had a lot of experience in the 30s and 40s bus-and-trucking it all over the country. He said, "Goldie, you can do whatever you want. I'll support you. But it's a hell of a life. You better be darned sure it's what you want to do because it'll toughen you up real quick."'

Goldie had always placed great store by her father's advice and thought long and hard about what he had said. Was she just swopping the grind that she had known in New York for one on the road which might also lead nowhere?

She decided to go back to Los Angeles. But she would give

47

herself just nine months to succeed – or else. 'I arbitrarily chose nine months. I told the guys, "If nothing happens to me by then, call me up and we'll get this act together."'

Although it was clearly just another gamble, Goldie says she had also realised she was temperamentally and morally unsuited for Las Vegas. 'So once again I grabbed Lambchop and we headed back to California. I had this hunch that Hollywood couldn't be worse.'

Goldie's hunch proved right. But she needed a touch of luck to add to her hard-won experience. And Lady Fortune smiled on her not once, but twice, almost as soon as she arrived in Tinsel Town.

'You know, I had no sooner got to LA than I got a TV show right off,' she says, with a shake of her head. And despite the fears that she nursed about the medium after her experience in Las Vegas, she was good enough on this show to be spotted by the man who was to launch her career on the way to stardom.

'The next thing I knew I was on a show with a 26-week guarantee with a part for me written in,' she also remembers. 'So I didn't take long. The nine months were never in it.'

Goldie's initial appearance was on the weekly *Andy Griffith Show* in which the country-style entertainer fronted comedy and song-and-dance routines. The eager, elfin-features and quite obvious dancing talent of Goldie Hawn seemed to leap out of the sketches in which she appeared.

They certainly leapt out of the TV set that Art Simon was watching. A shrewd representative of the huge William Morris Talent Agency, Art was not easily impressed by artists, old or new.

'But this girl certainly had something,' he was to remark later. 'She didn't look like the usual stereotyped chorus girl – and there was something so effervescent about everything she did.'

So impressed was Art Simon by Goldie's talent and what he saw as her potential, that he approached her directly about signing up with the Agency. She agreed, overjoyed, like a shot.

'He saw me,' Goldie says with quiet simplicity, 'signed me and pushed me.'

It was a meeting that was to change the course of her life.

As Art Simon had spotted Goldie on TV it was natural enough that the first audition he arranged was for another television show. But he was already convinced she had more potential than being just a dancer, and pushed her towards a new 'sit-com' series being produced by ABC called *Good Morning World*. The show was built around the lives of average Americans and their foibles. It was intended to be funny,

The face of an over-night TV phenomenon — *Laugh-In*'s 'dumb blonde.'

48

occasionally satirical, but basically 'soft centred' to use a media term.

Almost instinctively sensing where the show was at, Goldie armed herself with a very typically American prop for her audition. A coffee pot. It was a master stroke. Her comic routine with the pot delighted the producers and she found herself signed up to play a rather off-beat girl named Sandy.

'It was a "girl-next-door" part,' she says. 'Sandy was a bit of

'The character that came out on *Laugh-In* was a very special part of me.' Goldie with the hosts of the show, Dick Martin and Dan Rowan.

a kook, though. She got herself into silly situations quite unintentionally. And she had lines like, "I have go home now and get my roast out of the clothes dryer!"'

Goldie also has vivid memories of her first prolonged work before the television cameras. 'I remember my voice went up eight octaves the first time I spoke. I'd never had somebody put a clapboard in front of my eyes before and say, "Take One." When they did, my voice went way up, and suddenly I started talking in this high-pitched voice, which of course led to all the rest of everything. And of course when I heard people laughing at me I really liked it. Funny how things happen . . ."

Funny indeed. And it is funny to look back at the episodes of *Good Morning World*, for in Sandy there is something of the embryo character that Goldie was to develop with such stunning success in *Laugh-In*. But Goldie could have had no idea then she was taking the first steps towards becoming the 'Kooky Queen of American Comedy'.

While Goldie was working on the TV show, Art Simon also managed to secure her a small part in a film. It was only a small part, certainly, but it did mark her debut in films. Those dreams of Hollywood were taking on a certain reality.

The picture had the extraordinary title of *The One and Only Genuine Original Family Band* and was being made by the Walt Disney organisation. Goldie had been most appropriately cast as the 'Giggly Girl' and was listed way down at the end of the credits under her full name of Goldie Jeanne Hawn.

Based on the book, *The Family Band* by Laura Bower Van Nuys, the movie told the true story of the Bower family, a mother, father and eight children who formed themselves into a band to rally support for the Democratic Party during the 1888 Presidential Campaign. However, when the eldest daughter falls in love with a Republican newspaperman covering the campaign, some clever manoeuvring is required to prevent the band being destroyed by political rivalries. Despite featuring such talented stars as Walter Brennan, Buddy Ebsen and Lesley Ann Warren, the picture was to prove one of the few failures from the Disney studios. When it opened in March 1968, *Time* magazine declared scathingly that it 'could have been cut up and used for flypaper – and maybe ought to be.'

Perhaps understandably, Goldie has said little about her first experience at movie-making – and *The One and Only Genuine Original Family Band* has a tendency not to be listed in surveys of her work. But in 1968, while in something of a reflective mood with Andy Warhol, she did have this to say:

'I was the lead dancer in it. They called me the giggly girl. I

51

didn't say one word. In fact I looked for my part for three days.

'Finally, I called the studio. I said. "I think there's been a mistake here because I can't find my scenes." They said, "They're on page so-and-so." Well, of course they were all in the explanation. What are you supposed to do? Kick as high as you possibly can and keep your mouth shut!'

In fact the only thing that Goldie found at all memorable about the film was a young man she saw on the set called Kurt Russell. 'We looked at each other from across the room and I thought, "Gee, he's so cute."'

Though Goldie did not realise it then, destiny was to bring them together again almost seventeen years later . . .

Despite all the energy and invention that was put into *Good Morning World* – and the good critiques it received – its ratings did not reach a high enough level to satisfy ABC, and the show was dropped. Like all the performers Goldie was disappointed – but at least she had found the key to where her greatest success as an entertainer might lie: in comedy. How her future might have continued from that moment if *Good Morning World* had been allowed to continue can now only be a matter of conjecture.

But fate was about to play an even more dramatic hand in Goldie's life as the final episodes were screened. Watching these was another television executive named George Schlatter, the recently appointed producer for a new show to be assembled around the comic duo of Dan Rowan and Dick Martin to be called *Rowan and Martin's Laugh-In* (later shortened to *Laugh-In*).

Dan Rowan has explained the origins of the show. 'Dick and I had wanted to do a show like this for a long time. We felt it was impossible to depend on big name guest stars every week to get laughs. So we wanted a show in which we surrounded ourselves with talented and funny people who could improvise. But it took us a long time to convince anybody that it would work.'

Laugh-In had a quite different concept to *Good Morning World*, but as he watched the show, George Schlatter decided he wanted Goldie. Quite how he would use her in the mélange of zany humour developed through quick-fire sketches, jokes and one-line puns that was to make up the show, he was not sure. But he reckoned she had *something* he could use. Goldie, for her part, jumped at the chance. She was about to turn the key to stardom.

Goldie was just twenty-two and had only been in Hollywood a few months when she began work on *Laugh-In* during the weeks prior to its launching in January 1968. How the personality of the TV Goldie with her irrepressible giggle, delightful malapropisms and radiant, little-girl presence came about, is now a television legend.

George Schlatter tells it this way. 'We had no specific part for her to begin with,' he says, 'So we just let her dance to start with and she looked kinda cute. Then we decided to give her an introductory line to a sketch. Well, she blew it. Not once, but three times. And each time she broke into this embarrassed giggle. We all broke up, too.

'The third time the director gave the cut sign. But something hit me at that moment. "Never stop her again," I ordered. "Never. That is absolutely adorable."'

Goldie herself admits that the reason for her mistakes was because she was so nervous. She really had no idea why people were laughing. But George Schlatter had sensed that he had stumbled onto something that would delight audiences – now there was the challenge to make Goldie laugh spontaneously, not once but over and over again.

'Week after week we kept dreaming up fiendish new ways to distract her,' recalls Schlatter. 'We had meetings on the subject. "Okay, what are we going to do to Goldie that's really awful tomorrow night?" She knew something strange would happen – it always did – but she never knew what. Often we would switch the cue cards on purpose, or else the crew behind the camera would do things to distract her. Like make faces, or hold up dirty words.'

George Schlatter particularly remembers another crucial incident that happened just before the very first show was recorded.

'Goldie was a bit upset about the way some people were treating her. Thinking she was just a dumb blonde and nothing more. "George," she said to me, "Some of these people don't think I'm for real." I replied, "Don't worry, Goldie. Some of them think I am." To which she said, "Poor baby!" And as everyone knows that became one of her most famous catch-phrases!'

The show was, of course, an overnight smash success. In a matter of weeks it had earned a weekly viewing audience of 50 million viewers across America, pushing all opposition off the screen. This was soon to be repeated when *Laugh-In* crossed the Atlantic to Britain.

At the heart of the success was Goldie – the elfin-faced blonde who captured everyone's heart, men in particular. It was an astonishing achievement, turning her from an unknown into a personality far quicker than anyone – certainly she herself – could have believed possible.

Although there were, of course, instant judgements made

on what was the secret of her success, Goldie let time pass and distanced herself from this momentous change in her life before giving her own opinion. This is how she put it into perspective while talking to David Thomson in 1982.

'The character that came out on *Laugh-In* was me,' she admitted candidly. 'It was a very special part of Goldie. It wasn't dreamed up. I didn't sit at home and figure how I was going to turn those men on. I didn't figure any of it.

'The way it happened was quite naturally. You see when I get nervous I see things sometimes blurred and sometimes in reverse positions. I don't think I'm dyslexic – but when I look at a prompt card I have never seen before, and I'm also being made nervous by the lights and all that stuff, well, I skip round it. That was only in the beginning when I didn't really know why I was there. They were sort of giving me a try-out for three shows.

'Anyway, I started to laugh because I had messed it up. That's the way I am. I have never taken myself that seriously anyway, so I just got tickled by the whole thing. And then I'd look off the set, expecting them to stop the tape, but they didn't. So then I got sillier and *that's* a definite part of my character. It was funny. It worked. And she was charming.

'As time went on, I became more aware of what was happening and knew how to respond. If I had any problems at all, it was after two and a half years of doing the same thing over and over again. There were just no surprises left for me. I had to do exercises to get myself there. I had to empty my head of everything I knew – never looked at a script – and wait till the red light went on. And when it did, I just had to *go* for it. And that became very, very difficult.'

Of course, there were those who didn't like Goldie, who called her the 'ultimate dumb blonde' and that she was unashamedly 'catering to a very old-fashioned male sensibility'. Although *Laugh-In* had catapulted her to fame, she was not at a loss for words to defend herself.

Again she told David Thomson: 'I never resented my role. At that point in my career I never felt the strain of social feminine injustice. I was never involved with any suffering women who were in that kind of misery. And I had a job to do. Some people just lost their sense of humour and took it so far it was ludicrous!'

Such people were very much in the minority. For in a matter of a few months, Goldie was a household name, loved for the giggling, whipped-cream sense of fun she brought into the living rooms of America.

It was an incredible transformation of a one-time go-go dancer into a comedy star of whom her co-star Dick Martin soon proclaimed: 'She's the nearest thing to Judy Holliday in years.'

The comparison was an apt one indeed. For like Judy Holliday, Goldie was soon to experience all the highs and lows which overnight fame can bring.

3 America's Favourite Dumb Blonde

IN THE short space of just a few months in 1968 Goldie Hawn became America's favourite blonde comedienne. As a result of her effervescent performances on *Rowan and Martin's Laugh-In* she was soon the nation's number one favourite on magazine covers, in newspaper headlines and she was being quoted – or perhaps one should say misquoted – across the length and breadth of the country. Goldie-jokes soon put the perennial Irish cracker to shame. 'Even by American standards,' one newspaper wrote, 'her career has been meteoric.'

Feature writers and journalists as a whole had a field day over her arrival – and comparisons with the comedy style of the late Marilyn Monroe were as inevitable as they were obvious.

As far as Goldie was concerned the 'dumb blonde' she personified on the screen was something she was prepared to go along with in these early, whirlwind months. But she also wanted to get something else straight.

'People like to see me being all giddy and silly,' she told one interviewer,' and if it pleases them, then that's the way I'll appear. But that's *not* the end of it.

'I'm smarter than some people are giving me credit for,' she went on. 'I mean, I have moods and levels like anyone else. Sometimes I feel klutzy and girlish, other times I feel very sophisticated . . . not funny, just grown-up and womanly.'

Certainly she was grown-up in terms of her show business experience; and grown-up enough for the millions of male admirers she was winning week after week. What made her unique for them was not just her pert and pretty face or that trim little figure she displayed in a bikini on every show. It was the combination of all these features and her personality – a result that caused George Schlatter to remark that, 'You don't know whether to take Goldie to bed – or home to mother.'

'I remember my voice went up eight octaves the first time I spoke. And of course when I heard people laughing at me I really liked it.' Goldie in 1968.

Overleaf: Goldie — the pioneer of body graffiti — off duty but still in a bikini!

57

The bikini segment of the *Laugh-In* became one of its highlights: and was also a television first for which Goldie can take credit. Her appearances with one line jokes painted, graffiti style, across her body were a test for the viewer to see how many he could read. Particular favourites like, 'The Bermuda Triangle is a *ménage à trois*' and 'Colonel Saunders is Chicken' remain fixed in the mind to this day.

Her sketches could equally well convulse an audience:

Says a garage man to Goldie, 'Sorry, Miss, you've got a flat battery.'
To which Goldie replies: 'Oh, gee, what shape should it be?'

Goldie never allowed her character to stand still, striving week by week to show that she was innocent rather than dumb, gullible rather than stupid; as well as being joyous, naive and intensely feminine. She also refused to take more than her fair share of the credit for the success of *Laugh-In*.

Speaking of its success in hindsight she has said: '*Laugh-In* poked fun and vented anger. In the late 60s there was a lot going on, a lot of matters of concern that TV just wasn't telling like it was. The show found our faults and laughed at them. I think it emerged directly out of the repressed 50s and succeeded because of their inhibitions.'

It would be wrong, though, to think that Goldie did not make the most of the opportunity presented by the success of the show to promote her own career. She had, after all, worked too hard and struggled for too long to let the chance slip by.

She adopted a zany appearance in public – wearing a variety of colourful mini-skirts and crazy hats, for example – and would giggle her way mischievously through the seemingly endless interviews. In particular she delighted in giving 'dumb' answers to certain reporters she felt were totally insensitive.

'Will you make it in Hollywood?' one scribe had enquired. To which Goldie replied with open-mouthed astonishment, 'I've *never* been made in Hollywood!'

When she had been a dancer had she ever gone topless, another asked? 'Topless? *Me?*' she had giggled. 'I'm only thirty-four up here!'

And what were her plans for the future? 'To marry, have two children and settle in Oregon.' Why Oregon? 'Oh, it's magnificent,' she would smile. 'Haven't you been there? I haven't either.'

If she sometimes found such questioning hard to take seriously (though she got better headlines by *not* doing so) she

took the fan mail which poured in very much to heart. 'I get a lot of letters from people who can identify with my character,' she reported in November 1968. 'That's nice – and they can see that she is not so much stupid as childlike.'

There were many flattering ones – including several proposals of marriage. One, from England, said touchingly: 'You don't know who I am, Goldie. But I love you.'

In fact, though, love had already entered Goldie's life in the person of a dark, handsome 29-year-old Greek American named Gus Trikonis. Like her, Gus was a dancer and they had actually met two years earlier when both were appearing in the 'tent show' musical, *Kiss Me Kate*. Gus had subsequently gone on from this to land parts in two successful musicals, *Bajour* and *West Side Story* while Goldie had struggled – seemingly unavailingly – for her big break.

Gus, in fact, provided Goldie with her first solid relationship since she had left home. Like her, he aspired to being more than just a dancer – directing was his ultimate goal – and if fate had meant them to come together it could hardly have given them a better omen than the fact that they shared the same birthdate – November 21!

By nature a kind and sensitive man, Gus was an ideal person to be on hand when fame turned Goldie into a star overnight. He gave her support and reassurance and helped her keep her sense of perspective. From her point of view, Goldie loved the fact that she could slip away from the limelight each evening and spend the time quietly preparing for the next onslaught.

Neither were strongly attracted to the round of night clubbing and high-speed life style which most Hollywood stars adopted. They were happiest at home, and now that Goldie was beginning to earn real money at last, this went into investments and savings rather than ostentatious living.

The only thing that could be said in any way to be marring their otherwise ideal relationship was that Gus was enjoying nothing like the success of Goldie in his career . . .

By the Spring of 1969, Goldie who was now twenty-three, was declaring publicly that she had found the man she wanted to marry. 'I fell in love with Gus because he is strong, firm and determined,' she told writer John Sampson, 'and I want to be married because I need an honest relationship with a man. I don't want to be some kind of half-baked floozy who lives with whatever man interests her at the moment and then later goes on to someone else.'

Gus would beam at this and say simply, 'Goldie is so full of life. She is quick and clever, too.'

The couple got married in May in Honolulu. They slipped quietly away from Los Angeles and flew to Hawaii with only

Previous page: Goldie in London with husband Gus Trikonis not long after their marriage.

Mike Frankovich, the producer who launched Goldie in films at a Hollywood dinner in his honour in 1970.

Goldie's agent, Art Simon, for company. Neither informed their parents of the wedding because they were anxious to avoid the razzmatazz that would engulf the hottest new female star on television if news of the impending marriage got out. They wanted the event to be quiet, unpretentious and simple.

The actual ceremony took place in the couple's hotel, performed by a justice of the peace, with Art Simon as the only witness. Goldie plumped for informality in her wedding 'dress' – green silk hip-huggers and a huge gardenia in her tumble of blonde hair. Gus wore blue jeans and a sweater.

The transformation of Goldie Hawn to Mrs Goldie Hawn Trikonis was smooth and without complications: and almost before they knew it, the couple were Los Angeles-bound again where Goldie had another season of *Laugh-In* to begin taping. It had been one of the quietest star weddings on record.

Such was the public interest in Goldie now, however, that once her secret was out, she had to bow to demands from the press for a peep into the life she and Gus planned to make together. First they wanted to see the $75,000 New England-style house they had bought in the fashionable Los Angeles suburb of Bel Air. But it proved to be quite a surprise – for there were no evident signs of sudden wealth, no lavish fixtures and fittings or an array of servants. Just tasteful furniture, stylish decorations, the faithful poodle, Lambchop, a Hungarian sheepdog called Big Crunch and a Siamese kitten, Tricia.

'When I started out,' Goldie told a visiting writer from *Woman's Home Journal*, 'what I most wanted was to be a woman who married the husband she wanted and had the house she wanted. Now I have that.

'I'm actually a middle class sort of person,' she continued. 'And despite my success, what I want is to have a middle class kind of life. A nice house, get pregnant and raise a family. I couldn't stand the rich bit with flocks of servants and all that. I like cleaning up my home. Cleaning the floor, doing the dishes, then spraying the flower beds. My favourite activities are knitting, crochet, cooking, reading, listening to classical music like Bach and Beethoven, and making my own clothes.'

If Goldie sometimes giggled when she talked, it did not mean what she said was to be taken anything less than seriously. 'I know that may sound funny in a place like Hollywood, but this is the kind of lifestyle Gus and I like. I mean we live in a home not a hotel. We don't want servants because our privacy is too important to us.'

Goldie was also quick to tell writers about her husband's abilities as a painter of imaginative pastel pictures. And of his plans to be a film director.

Her first major screen role in *Cactus Flower* (1969) brought Goldie face to face with one of her screen idols, Ingrid Bergman.

'We're two different human beings pursuing different career goals,' she would say to any suggestion that her fame was overshadowing his. 'And what does it matter if one of us earns more money?'

Those were to prove very prophetic words.

There was little doubt that Goldie was anxious not to let fame change her. But equally both she and Art Simon – delighted that the little girl he had spotted was starting to fulfil all the potential he had seen in her – wanted to move her career on a step. She didn't want to just remain America's favourite TV 'dumb blonde' – even if she could have done – but open up new avenues. And the movies seemed the obvious choice.

Because of her success on *Laugh-In* – and because Hollywood likes nothing better than capitalising on someone's success in another medium – film companies were now sitting up and taking notice of Goldie Hawn. Her debut in *The One and Only Genuine Original Family Band* may not have set the world on fire, but she had come a long way on TV since then.

The *Los Angeles Times* broke the news of the next big step in her life. 'Producers are hurrying to the door of Goldie Hawn, the "vairy interesting but stupid" star of the smash-hit TV series, *Laugh-In*,' the paper noted on June 8, 1969. 'And now she's landed a plumb role to launch a career in movies. She's signed to co-star with Walter Matthau and Ingrid Bergman in Mike Frankovich's *Cactus Flower*.'

The delight at getting this part was heightened by the fact that she had long admired the irascible comic, Walter Matthau, and Ingrid Bergman had, of course, been an idol since her childhood. This pleasure spilled over when she talked to the press.

'I suppose I do come across as being silly,' she said. 'Men like it that way. It makes them feel superior. And they are – kind of. But silliness is only one part of me. Some people say I'm like Marilyn Monroe. I don't think so. But it's sweet of them to say so.'

The reference to Monroe was an interesting one. For behind the candy floss grin she was putting on in public, Goldie was beginning to feel some of the uncertainties which strike anyone in the aftermath of a success such as hers.

Later she was to reveal these uncertainties quite candidly. 'Everything happened so quickly with *Laugh-In* that there were times when I felt very insecure. I mean, before I had struggled for any kind of recognition, now suddenly I was being given all sorts of opportunities. There seemed to be no limits. It was all rather frightening.'

Goldie has also admitted that after a year of tumultuous acclaim on television there were times when she was 'terrified of being Goldie Hawn.' She felt her fame – and her fans – were going to overwhelm her. And she was worried, too, of falling into the trap of alcohol, drugs and casual sex which was such a common currency in Hollywood, and in particular a feature of so many success stories. She sensed that her success could become a tragedy under the awful pressures of fame.

There was Gus, of course. But she also needed to quieten her inner self as she came to terms with having gone from a small town girl who just wanted to be a dancer to a national celebrity recognised everywhere she went.

Goldie found her adjustment through psychoanalysis. She believes her decision to have therapy was a crucial one which ultimately helped her become balanced and happy in her new role in life. In fact, she saw her psychiatrist for seven years and is convinced this is how she ended up 'with my feet firmly on the ground'.

In discussing this period of her life with a writer in 1979 she summed it up thus: 'When you get fame and money you have to learn to protect yourself. I had to make sure I didn't lose my sense of values.'

It was perhaps because of the pressures and inner turmoil that she was feeling that Goldie brought such feeling to her role as Toni in her first major screen appearance in *Cactus Flower* which she filmed in the summer of 1969. Indeed, she confessed later, 'I understood the character, and maybe I was a little like her, too.'

Interestingly, it was that old maestro of the film-makers, Billy Wilder, who had spotted Goldie on television months before and recommended her to producer Mike Frankovich for *Cactus Flower*. She was aware of his influence and remains grateful to Wilder to this day.

'He was the first person to spot me when I was just a personality,' she says. 'He wanted me to work at my acting. He said he was sure that one day I would be able to tackle *any* part.' (It was also Billy Wilder, incidentally, who later encouraged Goldie to become a film producer.)

Mike Frankovich actually took little convincing about Goldie's potential and backed his judgement by offering Art Simon a four-picture contract for her services. After signing, Goldie told the press, 'I had thought that I'd try for films one day – but things have always come to me when I wasn't looking. Of course, you've also got to know how to use your luck!'

Good luck seemed to surround the picture from the start. The three stars got on famously – and Matthau, often less than patient with newcomers to the film business, was charmed by Goldie. 'She warms you inside, like a bowl of porridge with cream and honey on a winter day,' he commented. And Goldie

Overleaf: A moment of tranquillity in a busy life...

was deeply appreciative of his help and kindness. 'Walter reminds me of an uncle of mine,' she said. 'He never gets tired of putting me on. He even kept calling me "Goldala" which he knows I hate!'

The film's director, Gene Saks, was equally impressed with Goldie. 'Never has a girl in her first film been so professional,' he said. 'She was instant relaxation for all of us on the film.'

Goldie was, of course, very well aware of what an important step *Cactus Flower* was for her. 'It gave me a chance to prove that I had a heavy side,' she said later. 'The girl Toni was a very different character from the dopey blonde in *Laugh-In*. She had more depth and colour. I've always had a wide range of emotions, and being a sensitive person there's plenty for the actress in me to tap.'

Aside from its stars, the picture was also blessed with an excellent script by Billy Wilder's long-time associate, I. A. L. Diamond, based on Abe Burrow's successful stage play, and music by Quincy Jones.

The story centred around Matthau as Julian Winston, a free-wheeling bachelor dentist who wants to bed but not wed beautiful Goldie, and to prevent her getting ideas about marriage, invents a wife and three children. To sustain this deception, he has his secretary, Stephanie, played by Ingrid Bergman, pose as his wife. Complication inevitably piles on complication until the affair ends in a mixture of high drama and side-splitting hilarity.

Rarely can a comedy picture have been greeted by such critical enthusiasm as was *Cactus Flower*. For a start, *Time* magazine asked – and answered – what it called 'one of the most engaging questions facing America today – can *Laugh-In*'s Goldie Hawn really act?' Writing in the issue of November 11, 1969, film critic Jay Cocks decided, 'Yes, she can,' and he went on: 'Goldie is a natural reactress; her timing is so canny that even her tears run amusingly. In recent years Broadway comedies have not survived translation into film. Although unpretentious, *Cactus Flower* succeeds on screen, thanks to two old masters – and a shiny new one – who have learned that actors get known by the comedy they keep.'

Howard Thompson of the *New York Times* also spotlighted Goldie's contribution to the picture. 'It is mainly the emerging sweetness and perceptions of this girl's character, as an inquisitive Greenwich Village kook, that gives the film its persuasive lustre and substance,' he said.

And when *Cactus Flower* opened in Britain not long afterwards, the praise was just the same. Dick Richards of the *Daily Mirror*, for instance, wrote: 'Ever since TV's *Laugh-In*, anyone with an ear to a pub bar will have heard strong men drooling over the show's zany young kookie, Goldie Hawn. Now she makes her screen bow in *Cactus Flower* in which she sparkles as a sad-funny, cute, petite dish with a touch of Marilyn Monroe, Debbie Reynolds and Baby Doll.'

The *Morning Star* also supported Dick Richards's view, declaring that 'in her first major screen role, Goldie Hawn gives one of the best comedy performances of the year' while the *Sunday Express* was quite emphatic that she had 'proved herself a comedienne of limitless charms'.

But it was the *Daily Mail*'s Barry Norman – ever after a Goldie-fan – who really brought out the accolades. 'Through the years,' he wrote, 'the most sought-after screen actresses have always been the comediennes, the sexy ones who can make you laugh and still look desirable while doing it. Marilyn Monroe, for instance. Judy Holliday, Shirley MacLaine. Now add Goldie Hawn. For in her first film, *Cactus Flower*, she walks away with the whole thing. Simply steals it. Blatant, daylight robbery.

'For a start, she looks so fantastic – head like a beautiful mop, face that appears to consist solely of eyes, and rather more length of leg than it seems proper for one girl to possess. But then we knew all that before. The revelation here is that she really can act. Yes, but exactly *how* does she act?

'Well, she acts a bit like Marilyn Monroe (the same kind of outrageous innocence), and a bit like Shirley MacLaine (a similar brand of, for want of a better word, kookiness), and quite a lot like Judy Holliday (moments of such breath-taking, bird-brained dumbness that you want to keep her as a pet). Furthermore . . . no, on second thoughts, let's not get carried away and drag Charlie Chaplin into this too. And yet it must be said that she also has the born clown's gift of knowing precisely when to turn pathos into laughter.'

It was a stunning reception – and in Britain it naturally excited interest in her all the more when it was announced that she was crossing the Atlantic in January 1970 to make her second movie. A picture that was to team her up with another of the world's great comedians, England's own Peter Sellers, in *There's a Girl in My Soup*.

However, during the course of making *Cactus Flower*, Goldie had made a very important discovery about herself, which made another decision concerning her career imperative.

'I found that movies seemed to go better with my chemistry,' was how she put it. 'Doing a TV show every week is really hectic. You just don't have enough time to analyse your character. But in films you can *think* your role out. They are so much more fulfilling.'

The conclusion to be drawn from such thoughts was

obvious. She decided the time had come to quit *Laugh-In*. It was not, though, a decision taken lightly.

In many ways, Goldie was loath to even *think* about leaving the show that had made her a star as well as the people who had become more than fellow actors but friends. But somehow she knew that if she was to reap the benefit of all that she had learned on television – her unique sense of timing a joke, her skill at projecting the image of a zany character who could make audiences laugh uproariously, and most importantly her own belief in herself as an entertainer – then the time to move on was *now*: before she grew tired of the series or, more dangerously, viewers grew tired of her. Films beckoned and there would surely be a chance to try her hand at more serious acting: a challenge she could not resist or ignore if she wanted a really enduring career.

There were, though, tears in her eyes when she told producer George Schlatter her decision. 'It was a really traumatic moment,' she was to reflect later. 'I just howled on George's shoulder. It was like going away from home for good. But you have to make the break and once you've made it, you have got to stand by it.'

Sadly, the paths of Goldie and the other members of the *Laugh-In* team were destined never to cross again after she left in January 1970. And fate (that 'famous fickle finger of fate' to quote a *Laugh-In* catch-phrase) decreed that while great things lay in store for her, none of the others were ever to match her fame. Indeed, today she remains the best-known figure from the programme (a fact which does not always please her when mentioned, considering all her other achievements), and is still the one most eagerly looked for when the series is re-run. The fact that it can be, and is, re-run today, is surely the finest tribute to the durability of its humour.

Of the *Laugh-In* cast, Dan Rowan is now retired, while Dick Martin appears occasionally on TV game shows. Arte Johnson, Ruth Buzzy, Jo Anne Worley and Henry Gibson are here and there on television, but neither of the other two top comediennes, Lily Tomlin and Judy Carne have achieved the kind of media exposure their undoubted talents deserve. British-born Judy was, of course, for a time married to Burt Reynolds, who later starred in one of Goldie's most accomplished films, *Best Friends*, made in 1983. That same year Judy told Clive Hirschhorn rather wistfully of the different careers that fate had dealt them.

'I've got no one to blame but myself,' Judy admitted. 'I should have taken a lesson from Goldie Hawn who, as you know, also received her big break on *Laugh-In*. Goldie was just the opposite from me. She refused all the offers that

'Goldie warms you inside like a bowl of porridge with cream and honey,' Walter Matthau said of his co-star in *Cactus Flower*. And Goldie responded: 'Walter reminds me of an uncle of mine. He never gets tired of putting me on!'

weren't right for her – including a Coca Cola commercial for $100,000. She said no to chat and game shows, and when, finally, she left *Laugh-In* she went straight into the movies and hasn't looked back since.'

Although she couldn't have known at the time just how right she was to make the break, Goldie was taking the path which – as *Film Comment* was to say a decade later – 'changed her from being the tongue-tied resident comic pin-up of the TV show to become the most commercially consistent comic actress of recent years.'

But such a verdict was a long way from coming true in January 1970 when Goldie bid farewell to the show and flew to England to begin filming with Peter Sellers. Somehow, though, beneath the sadness she sensed things were on the move.

'For me it was the end of an era,' she was to say later, 'the end of part of my life. But I had a feeling it was the beginning of something even more exciting.'

Just how exciting she was to find out with very much the same remarkable speed that had greeted her debut in television.

Far left: Goldie looking stunning at the London premiere of *Cactus Flower* in March 1970.

Left: Goldie looking every inch a lady in two candid shots.

4 Pure Goldie

THERE WAS an extraordinary reception awaiting Goldie Hawn when she arrived in London on January 30 1970.

Laugh-In was, of course, already firmly established on British television as an immensely popular weekly show with an audience in excess of ten million. And Goldie, with her 'corn-coloured hair and child-like giggle' (as one TV critic had put it) was undoubtedly one of the favourites with viewers – women as well as men. This popularity had naturally generated considerable press interest in her visit to make a movie with Peter Sellers based on London's long-running stage comedy, *There's a Girl in My Soup*.

The *Daily Mail* newspaper stole a march on its rivals by sending its film critic Barry Norman – who, of course, had raved over *Cactus Flower* – to catch her in Paris where she had made a stop-over during her flight from California. Always a verbal wizard, Barry did not disappoint his readers in a story datelined 'Paris, Wednesday, January 29.'

'Goldie Hawn arrives in London tomorrow,' he wrote, 'a rare treat for the local citizenry since it will afford them a glimpse of a species that is now, alas, almost extinct – namely, the dumb blonde. And Miss Hawn, as followers of *Laugh-In* will know, is a blonde of such dizzy dumbness as to induce severe boggling of the mind. Indeed, the most notable thing about her is not that she looks as if she had been drawn by a sexually motivated Disney artist, nor even that her legs appear to begin under her ears, but that she is unmistakably dumb. "I guess," she said over lunch today on the Champs-Elysées, "that's why everything is happening to me!"'

But as almost everyone was coming to appreciate, Barry knew that the dumbness was just an act. 'I cannot see,' he ended his report, 'how she can possibly escape the kind of gilt-edged international stardom that Marilyn Monroe enjoyed.'

'A species that is now almost extinct — the dumb blonde.' Goldie with Peter Sellers in *There's a Girl in my Soup*. (1970).

77

When Goldie arrived at Heathrow the following day a large press contingent was waiting. Her zany image and whether she worried about being presented this way, was inevitably foremost in the journalists' questions.

'No, it doesn't bother me,' she said brightly, 'because it's nice to be cheerful and friendly, and anyway, anything else is not worthwhile.' And she repeated what she had said before, 'The silliness is just part of me. I believe if I tried to be funny, I wouldn't be. I don't have that kind of humour that would make me quick on the repartee. I can't come up with witty replies. But people seem to laugh at the things I say. Then I get the giggles.'

Had her fame changed her? 'I'm the sort of girl who can go out and buy a one hundred dollar dress and a one dollar lipstick and be more excited about opening the lipstick than the dress box,' she replied.

Several of the journalists wanted to know how she had developed the sense of comedy timing which had been such a feature of her *Laugh-In* appearances. 'I honestly don't know the answer,' she said. 'but it must have some connection with my training as a dancer. Whenever I am playing any sort of part, I hear the beat in my head and just speak the lines in rhythm with it.'

Naturally, she was looking forward to the challenge of making *There's a Girl in My Soup* and working with Peter Sellers. 'It's so totally different from anything I have ever done and calls for some real acting to a challenging degree. It is something I never dreamed I would do and it's very exciting,' she added.

The reporters were captivated. 'Goldie is pure gold,' one wrote, 'gold in name, gold to look at, pure gold at heart and obviously worth her weight in gold as an actress.' The *Sunday Express*'s veteran Roderick Mann – not given to being impressed with American over-night stars – admitted in his column, 'I must confess that Goldie is a knock-out girl. Honest as a child's stare and full of fun and giggles. She's a true somebody and unless the portents are very wrong, Goldie the giggler is going to be a big, big star.'

The first major portent of stardom was, in fact, just a few days away after Goldie had begun work at Shepperton Studios with Peter Sellers and director, Roy Boulting.

In the film she was cast as a very blasé 19-year-old American girl who outsmarts Sellers as a forty-ish television show host with an unquenchable appetite for sex and a usually successful 'love-'em-and-leave-'em' technique. Although there were certainly elements of playing the madcap in Goldie's role as Marion, she also had to prove herself able to handle the mixture of shrewdness and skittishness the part demanded.

The chemistry between the master comic actor Sellers and the comparative newcomer was soon evident on the film set. Peter Sellers found Goldie delightful. 'I think everyone gets to love Goldie because in the fullest possible meaning of the word she is so nice,' he said.

Goldie was equally full of admiration for her co-star. Some years later she was to say, 'Working with Peter Sellers was one of the high points of my career. He didn't criticise or treat me like a novice as some people said he would. He was an extraordinary man and a great talent, and someone I found very complicated, very inspiring and very, very funny. He had a marvellous sense of humour on the set. There were times when we were laughing so hard that we'd have to break for lunch. There was no way we could do the scene.

'Peter told the most marvellous stories about his life and

'Working with Peter Sellers was one of the high points of my life...There were times when we were laughing so hard we had to break for lunch.' Goldie and her co-star having fun at Shepperton Studios.

talked a lot about Sophia Loren. He seemed to have loved her a lot. Yes, he was complicated. All actors are schizophrenic. It's just that some of us don't know it. Some hide it and just call on it for a part. But I found Peter to be very consistent in his attitude towards humour and towards his constant search for a place where he could live in peace. Peter was very high-strung and he knew it.'

Because of Peter Seller's well-known reputation for falling in love with his leading ladies, there were rumours during the making of *There's a Girl in My Soup* that he had fallen for Goldie. He may well have been the first of her leading men to have been strongly attracted to her – but he was certainly not going to be the last. Goldie, though, was never sure how deep the fated actor's affection ran.

'I really don't know if he fell in love with me,' she said of the rumours, a short while ago. 'I only know that I gave him a surprise party in my home some time after the film. He spent all evening looking at my things and said, "This is the kind of house I've always dreamed of having, with all the warmth and stability that I feel here.' Afterwards he sent me this absolutely gorgeous armoire which I still have in my home.'

Although director Roy Boulting was not aware of any romance between his stars, he was quick with his praise for Goldie as an actress. 'She has impressed me more than any other artist I have worked with in many years,' he said. 'She has an instinctive and immediate understanding of what is required. She not only has a great comic gift, but is capable of enormous dramatic depths. She shines with human warmth that is quite irresistible. I think she is going to be one of the great stars of the next decade.'

Support for Roy Boulting's opinion actually came before the picture was completed. On the morning of February 16, Goldie was suddenly awoken in her hotel bedroom in London by the sound of a telephone ringing. She remembers the incident vividly.

'I'm a deep sleeper,' she says, 'and it was some moments before I came awake. I looked at the clock beside my bed and thought, "What idiot is ringing me at 6 am?"'

When Goldie lifted the receiver she heard a voice crackling with excitement. It was Art Simon calling from California.

'Goldie,' he said, 'you've got an Oscar!'

Goldie was awake in an instant. She shot upright in bed and asked her manager to repeat what he had said.

'It's true,' the voice crackled again across 5,000 miles, 'they've given you Best Supporting Actress for *Cactus Flower*!'

Goldie remembers that for a moment she was stunned, then amazed, and finally gave one of her famous giggles. She knew

'She impressed me more than any other artist I had worked with in many years' Roy Boulting directing Goldie and Sellers in *There's a Girl in my Soup.*

Overleaf: Goldie with her first husband, Gus Trikonis, in 1969.

80

that she had been nominated for the award, but never for a moment thought she would get it. 'I couldn't believe it. It was only my second picture. My performance was just a drop in the bucket, I thought. But I *had* worked hard.'

The award was certainly no mean achievement for someone so new to the movies. And to win it, she had edged out several well-established actresses who had also been nominated, including Susannah York, Sarah Miles and Dyan Cannon.

The excitement of the Oscar kept Goldie on a high for days, and she was delighted with the bouquet of flowers that Peter Sellers presented to her on the set on behalf of everyone making the picture. To the press, she also revealed a curious piece of presentiment about the award.

'It concerns my mother,' Goldie said. 'She always had faith in me. When I telephoned her originally to tell her I'd got the part in *Cactus Flower*, she said, "Goldie, you're going to win an award for that." I said, "Oh, *sure!*" So when I did win the Oscar, she sent me a telegram which said, "Now when your mother tells you something – listen!"'

After all the delight at her out-of-the-blue Oscar had died down, Goldie was able to speak objectively about the impact it had upon her.

'It didn't really turn my head,' she said, 'because long before I won it, I had thought of my career as simply a job. When you start as a dancer, as I did, you have a different dream to a person who wants to be a movie star. I wanted to be a good dancer, and I wanted to work. And that was it. I didn't have any delusions of grandeur. When I've had a part in a picture or a TV show, I've looked at it as work. Part of that attitude may be self-preservation and part of it is the truth.

'I suppose in my heart I felt the Oscar was a little bit of deceit. I always thought you had to work for years and years to win an Academy Award and I didn't,' she added.

One thing that the award couldn't do was change her immediate plans. She had a four-picture deal already signed with Mike Frankovich – of which she was now on the second – so the immediate future would take care of itself.

What she hadn't banked on was the surprise which Roy Boulting greeted her with on the set one morning. He told her in a very matter-of-fact way that he wanted her to play a nude scene!

It was to prove another incident from the early days of her career that Goldie still remembers with engaging clarity.

'We were well into the schedule when I was suddenly informed that for the next scene in the bedroom, I was expected to be in the nude,' she says. 'But, gee, what can a girl do? If you say no everyone is going to get twitched up. But if

Bubbly blonde meets super stud — Goldie with Warren Beatty making *The Heist* (1971), which marked the beginning of their friendship.

85

you know all about it before the contract is signed, then you don't get caught with your pants down. Oops, you know what I mean! You're forewarned aren't you?

'So I agreed, but with a compromise. I refused to play the actual lovemaking scene in bed nude. I don't see why it's necessary to strip completely to bounce around under a sheet. It's not that I've got any hang-ups about nudity . . . but it's my close friends I feel for. They're the ones who'll get embarrassed.

'Afterwards, I wrote if off as a great lesson in film acting. The lesson being to make sure before you start shooting just what is expected of you in those bedroom scenes!'

Of the picture as a whole, Goldie found working in Shepperton 'less panicky' than Hollywood.

'Shooting there is at a more comfortable pace,' she said, 'which I like. The nice thing is that the British film-makers have a great respect for actors and refer to them as artists.

'Although I did not find the coldness that is regarded as traditionally British, I did find both the men and women – particularly the men – rather reserved. I like the American relaxed and down-to-earth attitude, but I imagine the world would be a dull place if we were all the same. Apart from the nude bit it was a great experience and I learned a lot from Roy Boulting,' she added.

It was, in fact, the 'nude bit' that later delighted several of the critics including Jack Bentley of the *Sunday Mirror* who called it 'the most delightful I've seen since film producers started trying to put the wardrobe department out of business.' He thought Goldie's performance was 'a superb piece of acting' and felt that Peter Sellers had 'regained his magnificent flair for observational comedy which has not been seen since *I'm All Right Jack.*'

Alexander Walker of the *Evening Standard* was also enthusiastic about the partnership. 'Watching Sellers and Goldie Hawn, as the American bird he tries to take to bed and ultimately is forced to take as wife (or almost), is to see a *pas de deux* of two comedians each of whom has divine timing, instinctive feel for a situation and a sharp eye open lest the partner win a trick,' he said. 'For Goldie Hawn it's confirmation that she's inherited a tradition of blonde dumbness I thought had died with Marilyn Monroe.'

And *Film Review* put the icing on the cake with a simple but emphatic statement that Goldie 'is the girl most likely to fill the gap left so sadly by the untimely deaths of Judy Holliday and Marilyn Monroe.'

To add to the pleasure of these reviews – and her Oscar – Goldie picked up another three awards in America for *Cactus*

Goldie out and about in the film world — here seen at the premiere of *Marooned*, starring Gregory Peck.

Overleaf: Goldie lightheartedly shaping up for a fight over the 'nude' scene with Peter Sellers in *There's a Girl in my Soup.*

Flower. The influential New York Film Critics Circle put her in fourth place in their poll for Best Supporting Actress, while the National Association of Theatre Owners (no doubt delighted at the way she was pulling paying customers into their cinemas) gave her the award as Female Star of the Year. And to top this off she received a special prize for her performance from the judges at Italy's prestigious Taormina Film Festival.

What a sudden galaxy of awards for a girl who had not so long before been glad of a few dollars for dancing on table tops!

When Goldie returned to America after finishing *There's a Girl in My Soup* her next assignment may well have given her a strong sense of *déjà vu*. For despite her reservations about TV, she agreed to appear in a fifty-minute special, *Burlesque is Alive and Well and Living in Burbank*, playing a sexy night club dancer! Described as a 'sizzling chunk of 1920s showbiz when rude comics flourished and built-like-crazy strippers ruled the tassel-twirling waves', it featured Goldie as a young striptease artist who has to parade before rows of leering men.

But unlike her previous real experiences, Goldie this time found her bump-and-grind routine greeted with loud cries of 'Aaaah – isn't she sweet!' It was a set-up, of course, but made quite an impact on the viewing audience. The TV critics as well.

'That off-beat, against-the-odds moment is more proof that Miss Hawn, beside owning the shrewdest empty head in North America, is a genuine show-business original,' declared the *New York Times*. 'The paradox being that Goldie is the sex symbol who inspires nothing but the nicest feelings. Vandals don't scribble rude remarks on her picture. They inscribe 'I Love Goldie' and leave it at that. How does she do it? By being her own woman and seeing right through modern hang-ups. They are there, she says, to be ignored. "Sexy?" she squeaks. "I'm not sexy. 'I'm married!'"'

The *Chicago Tribune* reviewer saw her as a 'sex symbol audiences dream of protecting instead of picking-up' and added that probably only Goldie could make sense of the contradiction. 'Being funny, often between or en route to some man's bed, is Miss Hawn's line of work,' the paper said. 'She does it supremely well – but her life is something else again. Audiences sense this, and respect her for it, even as they chuckle or dream. Which could be why the world is rushing into a fervent but strictly platonic love affair with Mrs Gus Trikonis.'

Despite such fulsome praise, Mrs Trikonis was determined *not* to let herself get carried away. Show business entre-

preneurs clamoured for her services in future films, on more television shows, in advertising commercials, and even to give concerts in Las Vegas. (And how *those* offers warmed her long suffering dancer's heart!) But neither they, nor the fans who clamoured to see her, nor the journalists and photographers who wanted to feature her in their publications, were going to change her.

'This year, with the Oscar and all, has been a magic time,' she grinned in December 1970, 'but I'm not sure I want to get used to it. I try to keep aware of myself at all times. The difficulty is that people put you in a position because of their own needs, so they make you all-important. But you have to understand that, and know that's false. Then, if you keep a cool head and a proper sense of values, you'll be all right.'

Goldie's 'proper values' were a nice home 'because that's where the biggest portion of my life is', lots of time with Gus, and entertaining their mixed circle of friends. Her 'career dynamic' – as she put it – was supplied by her manager because she felt she had 'virtually drifted' to where she was now.

'Unfortunately,' she said, 'I think the drifting days are over now, because when you are getting a regular influx of offers, decisions as to whether to go this way or that have to be made. But I never sit and dream that I've had enough comedy and that I must get my teeth into something more substantial. It may sound frivolous, but if I spent all my time deeply concentrating on my career, I'd end up in a sanatorium.'

She was, though, anything but frivolous about one future objective she held.

'I'm sure that the ultimate fulfilment will be to have children,' she said. 'I think that's when I shall feel really fulfilled. If my career is going to continue as it is at present, this is going to need a bit of planning. Pregnancy can play havoc with continuity on a movie that's six months in the making and I don't suppose the medical profession will come up with instant families in my lifetime.'

In the light of the way her relationship with Gus was to develop, these were to prove fateful words indeed. . . .

January 1971 saw Goldie flying back to Europe to make her third film, *The Heist* (also known as *$* or *Dollars*) which co-starred her with one of the great male sex symbols of the era, Warren Beatty. At first sight it looked like a box office certainty: the meeting of the bubbly blonde and the super stud. But things didn't quite work out that way.

Warren was cast as Joe Collins, an American security expert, who decides to reverse his role by trying to beat an

Previous page: 'Do you think there's a link between sex and crime?' One of Goldie's best moments from *The Heist.*

92

apparently fool-proof burglar system he has just installed in an exclusive West German bank. Goldie played Dawn Divine, a prostitute who becomes his partner in the 'heist' by telling him of the illegal deposits of money three of her clients have put in the bank. Both feel safe in the knowledge that none of these men dare complain to the police when their ill-gotten gains are stolen. It seems like the perfect crime. . . .

Sadly, despite all the ballyhoo that greeted the making of *The Heist*, it failed woefully to live up to expectations. Even though Columbia Pictures had gone to the trouble of transforming Hamburg's spectactular Kunsthalle (art museum) into the United World Bank (with a donation to the museum of $27,000 for the purchase of works of art) and handed the directing to the veteran Richard Brooks, the critics found it too long, too noisy, and the chase sequence which made up the finale too absurd. Jay Cocks of *Time* magazine thought it 'slow and confusing' and accused both Warren Beatty and Goldie of over-acting.

Mark Russell-Sean of the *Sunday People* also didn't like the picture, but did have a few kind words for Goldie. 'Mournfully watching yet another screenful of grim-faced hoodlums in yet another crime movie,' he wrote, 'my most charitable thought was. . . . Thank God for Goldie Hawn. If it wasn't for giggly Goldie's anti-yawn charm, *The Heist* would have been hard pressed to keep me from wandering off to the cinema's ice-cream lady for a lolly.'

Alexander Walker, who had so enjoyed Goldie in *There's a Girl in My Soup* again found her performance the only saving grace of the picture. 'But I'll forgive it everything because of Goldie Hawn as the peanut-brained accessory,' he said. 'Any man would break into a bank for her: to break into a bank *with* her must give one the kind of sensation she transmits so hilariously when she takes one look at a bundle of dollars, shuts her eyes in ecstasy for a second and then asks breathlessly, "Do you think there's a link between sex and crime?"'

Walker's disappointment was all the keener because he had expected a 'Big, Important Film' only to find a 'Highly Confused One'. Goldie, too, shared these feelings.

'I thought it was going to be a big picture,' she reminisced years later. 'It smelled like a hit, what with Warren and a robbery and me playing a prostitute. But it was a total bust. I can't look at the picture now. I've seen it one and a half times, and the second time I saw it, I had to turn it off.'

Despite her disappointment, Goldie had learned some more important lessons about film making from her work on *The Heist*. 'When you're starting out in the film business,' she told an interviewer, 'you accept people's advice. I was talked into

Overleaf: Moment of truth for Goldie when she realises the boy she thought was a 'Peeping Tom' is actually blind. A scene from *Butterflies are Free* (1972).

doing ridiculous things. You're malleable. You're an actor, an object, an instrument. And until you learn for yourself what's right and what's wrong, you listen to everybody but yourself. You're seduced by your director and later you say, "Why did I do that? I didn't want to do that."'

On the plus side, there had been the start of a friendship with Warren Beatty – which has lasted to this day – and the feeling that one day she would like to produce her own movie. An objective which, as we shall see, she ultimately realised.

Though the box office failure of *The Heist* was still in the future when Goldie flew back to America, she did not let any presentiments about it interfere with her next project – another television spectacular in which she was to be the star. *Pure Goldie* also gave her the pleasure of being reunited with her old *Laugh-In* companion, Ruth Buzzi. TV compere Johnny Carson was another guest.

Goldie was featured in several special segments including a production number which recalled her days as a chorus singer, a comedy sketch about an aeroplane so vast it contains a swimming pool and a barbeque pit, and a medley of the Beatles' hit songs. Once again the TV critics loved her.

'Goldie must be the brightest dumb blonde on the screen,' said *Newsweek*, adding: 'The confused lines that won her fame on *Laugh-In* were in fact all carefully studied. And last night we saw just how undumb she really is!'

There was careful study, too, that went into her next film, for Goldie was determined to reclaim any ground she might have lost in her career through the failure of *The Heist*. The movie was *Butterflies Are Free*, her fourth and final contracted picture for Mike Frankovich.

Goldie played Jill, a sexy, somewhat amoral aspiring actress living in San Francisco, who awakens one morning to find a young man staring into her apartment from another flat. As she is dressed in only a bra and panties beneath her flimsy nightgown, she naturally assumes the boy to be a Peeping Tom. Contemptuously she throws open her robe and pokes out her tongue. But the young man continues to stand and stare.

Jill's irritation is mixed with a kind of curiosity that someone can remain unmoved at such a display, and so she goes to the boy's flat – only to discover to her horror that he is blind. And has been so since birth.

From this traumatic enounter there develops a relationship which ultimately helps the boy Don (played by Edward Albert, son of the famous Eddie Albert) sever his dependence from an overbearing mother (Eileen Heckart) as well as making Jill confront the realities of her life for the first time.

Butterflies Are Free was, in fact, based on a true story – that of a blind young American named Harold Krents, who overcame his handicap to such a point that he could take a degree at Oxford, write a book, and develop such a social awareness that he was able to convulse a roomful of people with his wit and repartee. His achievement so caught the imagination of playwright Leonard Gershe that he used it as the inspiration for a play which captivated the hearts of Broadway audiences for a record 660 performances. This he then adapted for the film directed by Milton Katselas.

Goldie was enthusiastic about her part from the start. 'Jill is the most wonderfully written character,' she told a journalist in Hollywood, 'and her relationship with Don is beautifully written, too. Each day I look forward to going to work.'

This mixture of enthusiasm and ease with the part was translated into a film which was as critically well-received and financially successful as *The Heist* had not been. It was a most satisfying turnabout.

Tom Costner of *The Village Voice* lead the rave reviews in America. 'The audience at Radio City Music Hall loved it all,' he wrote, 'and throughout the film they were applauding or hissing at just the right moment.' The *New York Post* chipped in with: '*Butterflies Are Free* is a love story that could teach *Love Story* a thing or two. Both set out to play on the heartstrings. Both use blatantly emotive subjects to get their affects. But while *Love Story* nauseated, *Butterflies* succeeds magnificently.'

In Britain, the praise was similarly fulsome. 'I left the cinema with a warm feeling that comes from seeing a difficult theme beautifully handled,' said Felix Barker of the London *Evening News*. 'And how often can one say that?' Ken Eastaugh of the *Sun* underlined the point. 'This is no maudlin, sentimental melodrama,' he wrote. 'It has some of the wittiest lines you'll hear in any film.'

Donald Zec of the *Daily Mirror* who had been following the project from the beginning, was probably the most enthusiastic of all. 'It is a gem of a picture,' he declared, 'not only because the skinny, and not noticeably overclad Miss Hawn gives an intelligent, remarkably wide-ranging display of acting. Nor is it merely because it introduces a new young actor Edward Albert, who, on this showing alone has stimulated talk of "a new Paul Newman". What enriches this picture is the touching, ingenious and deadly-accurate way it deals with blindness. The success of *Butterflies Are Free* is due precisely to its skill in proclaiming that nothing embarrasses a blind person more than other people's embarrassment.'

And in a final reference to Goldie he added, 'She has finally

Previous page: Goldie with her co-stars in *Butterflies are Free*: Edward Albert, and Eileen Heckart as his over-protective mother.

Goldie once again giving her fans that 'Golden Feeling'.

switched from that unrelenting diet of bubble and squeak. Grudgingly the critics have conceded that behind all that unzipped flapdoodle there just might be an actress struggling to get out. Any further reluctance will be stunningly bowled out by *Butterflies Are Free*.'

Clearly a landmark had been reached in Goldie's career. The butterfly had emerged from her chrysalis as a fully fledged actress. And now that her contract with Mike Frankovich was complete, she and Art Simon were free to take their pick of the many offers to hand.

If any further proof of Goldie's arrival was needed, husband Gus was commissioned to answer them by writing and directing a TV film about her meteoric rise called *This Is My Wife*. Mrs Trikonis told the press how pleased she was.

'I actually put my husband before my career,' she confided to one writer, Philip Phillips. 'I'm a good cook and housewife, and I like gardening. If Gus told me to pack up my career, I'd do so immediately.'

Gus evidently had no intention of doing any such thing at that moment. But their marriage was certainly beginning to feel the first strains. And seen today, *This Is My Wife* is a rather poignant study, for as Goldie's success grows ever more unbounded, so one can sense Gus's becoming painfully restricted. Indeed, the signs of what the future held are there for all to see. . . .

5 A Journey to Despair

THE SUCCESS of *Butterflies Are Free* with both the critics and at the box office gave Goldie a tremendous sense of satisfaction. For in the picture she had really proved the range of her talent – that she could play drama without maudlin affectation, pathos without sickly sentimentality, and zany humour without resorting to the giggly dumbness with which she had become so closely identified.

In the picture which she made the following year, however, she shattered forever any stereotyped image the public might still have of her. In *The Sugarland Express* she gave a performance as a poor Southern girl – a 'piece of white trash' as one description put her – that was raw, gutsy, deeply felt and compulsively watchable. It was a performance the like of which had not been seen since the young Bette Davis had burst on the screen. If the movie was important for Goldie, so it was for the young director, a man who has since gained an immense international reputation – Steven Spielberg.

Spielberg, today acclaimed everywhere for movies like *Jaws, Close Encounters of the Third Kind* and the phenomenally successful, *E.T.*, was just twenty-six when he was offered his Hollywood debut with this picture by producers Richard D. Zanuck and David Brown. Though still so young, Spielberg had already directed a highly inventive episode of the television series, *Colombo*, and caused something of a sensation with a made-for-TV film called *Duel* about the relentless pursuit of a motorist by a seemingly driverless lorry. The sheer gripping intensity of the picture as the malevolent vehicle bears down on its prey held audiences spellbound when it was first shown – and still does today.

Left and Overleaf: Two angles on the same moment of light relief in *The Sugarland Express.*

Having graduated so spectacularly through the demanding school of television, Spielberg eagerly seized upon the chance to make a full-length feature film – taking a true story about

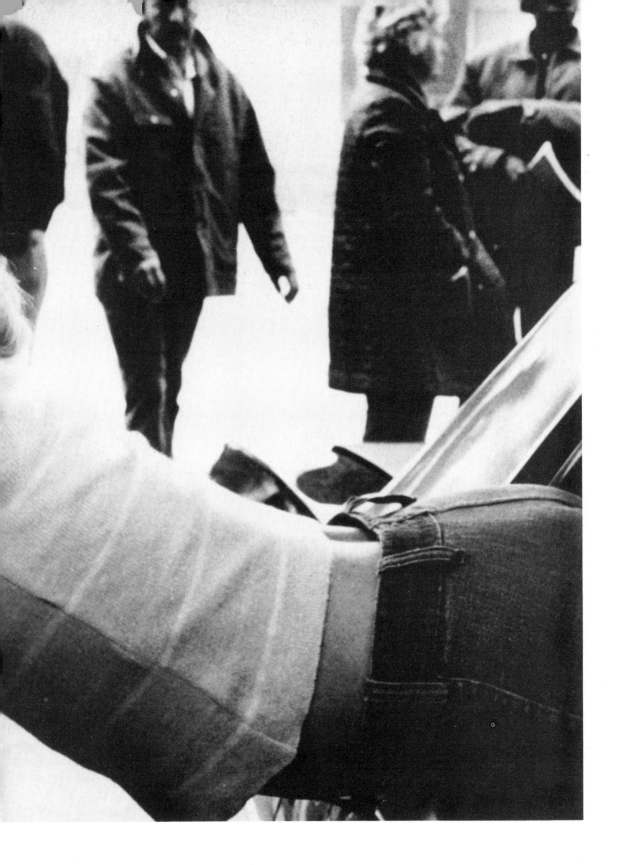

another kind of pursuit which had occurred in Texas in May 1969. He actually co-authored the script with Hal Barwood and Matthew Robbins and filmed the picture on the location of the original tragic events.

At the centre of the story is Lou Jean Poplin, a child-like Texas girl whose baby son has been taken from her by the State Authorities of California when she was put in prison for shoplifting. Her husband, Clovis, a mild-mannered, largely inneffective man, is also in prison, nearing the end of a sentence for petty theft. As soon as Lou Jean is released she visits Clovis determined to have him break out so that they can regain custody of their child who is now being looked after by foster parents in the town of Sugarland. Once Clovis had escaped from prison, the couple's odyssey across Texas begins.

To aid their escape, the couple commandeer a police car – complete with driver, Officer Slide – and holding him at gunpoint force him to take them to Sugarland. Though they are quickly tailed by other lawmen, such is the dedication to the sanctity of life of the chief officer, Captain Tanner, that he will not take the easy option of trying to kill them and thus end the pursuit.

As the entourage crosses the yawning miles of Texas a strange affinity grows up between the couple and Officer Slide – just as the posse of cars in pursuit grows ever larger and the interest in the saga brings people to the roadside in every little town they pass through. The almost inevitable finale which results in Clovis's death, Lou Jean's bewildered anguish at being no closer in retaining her child, and Officer Slide's despairing sympathy for them both, is deeply moving.

The quality of Spielberg's picture lay not only in the acting of his principals, but in his inventive use of the camera (some of the images can be seen in hindsight as direct forerunners to some of the most effective moments in pictures like *Close Encounters* and *E.T.*) and in his handling of what is surely one of the most spectacular car chases ever seen on the screen. With over 5,000 extras and almost as many cars, the shots of the seemingly endless lines of vehicles stretching away to the horizon alternately shimmering in the hot sunlight or dancing like red sparks in the night, are unforgettable.

The doyenne of American film critics, Pauline Kael was one of the first to herald the importance of the picture. Writing in the *New Yorker* of March 18 1974, she said it marked the 'debut of a new-style, new generation Hollywood hand'.

'Spielberg could be that rarity among directors, a born entertainer,' she went on, 'perhaps a new generation's Howard Hawks. In terms of the pleasure that technical assurance gives

an audience, this film is one of the most phenomenal debut
films in the history of the movies . . . Spielberg has a knack
for bringing out young actors and a sense of composition that
almost any director might envy.'

Of the cast, Ms Kael singles out William Atherton's Clovis,
Michael Sacks as Officer Slide and Ben Johnson as Captain
Tanner, but reserves her biggest appreciation for Goldie,
whose previous film roles she had evidently disliked!

'Probably everybody knows how talented Goldie Hawn is,'

Previous page: A complete change of role for Goldie in *The Sugarland Express* (1974) playing 'a piece of white trash'.

Left: Director Steven Spielberg at work on his first major movie with his stars, Goldie, William Atherton and Michael Sacks.

Right: Another off-duty picture of Goldie which catches her gaiety and charm.

she wrote, 'and that has made her screen performances the more disappointing. She's done darting, fidgety little bits of business in several roles, but she was stymied; she was thrashing around in tightly blocked pictures. Here you don't see her yanking the director's sleeve and asking, "Now?" She just does it. Spielberg's youth and speed release her; she stays in character, and the character grows. Lou Jean has more gumption than brains; she's the American go-getter gone haywire.'

Jon Landau of the influential *Rolling Stone* magazine also spotlighted what he called Goldie's 'effective performance'. He was another critic who had been won over.

'Spielberg,' he wrote, 'has made a movie about people he

likes and he shows understanding for the funny, frustrating and finally saddening choices that each must make. The four people are all doing the best they can and so the film's final sense of despair comes from our realisation that their best isn't good enough.

'That despair arises from Lou Jean's inevitable collision with a world she truly can't comprehend. She cares about her child only as a means of hanging onto her own childhood. And like an infant, she is reckless, irresponsible and demanding. No one, least of all her husband, who cheerfully follows her most bizarre whims, contests her, Her blindness to the consequences of her actions, for him as well as for her, coupled with her sudden awakening to the harm she has done, provides the film with its most moving quality.'

British critics were likewise moved by the picture. Charles Brewster of the *Morning Star* called it 'a cinematic event not to be missed' while the *Guardian*'s Derek Malcolm thought it 'a superior road movie . . . in which Goldie Hawn is at once funny, sad and real – a far cry from the aggressively kookie charmer of previous films.'

Despite the praise that was accorded to *The Sugarland Express* – although there were, to be fair, some dissenting voices – it failed to achieve the massive popularity that was expected of it. Zanuck and Brown had hoped for a major launching when it was first screened at the Cannes Film Festival, but had to be content with the Best Screenplay Award. This put Steven Spielberg in the curious position of being advised that he might make a better screenwriter than director!

Goldie, though, had no doubt about the importance of the picture. 'I think it was my finest performance,' she told an interviewer in 1980. 'It was the most rewarding work I had done . . . I sometimes try to understand why the movie wasn't more popular. It was Steven Spielberg's first feature and he was obviously talented. I think if there was a problem with the film it was that it was too serious, too unrelenting and too uptight.'

But this said, her touching, pathetic and at times highly dramatic performance as surely established her as an *actress* as it pointed to the success that lay ahead for Steven Spielberg as a director. No matter what *anyone* might say!

'I don't do any extensive tearing down of a character until I get right onto the set and see and feel what is happening.' An informal shot of Goldie working on *The Sugarland Express*.

The particular demands of the picture not surprisingly caused Goldie to give some very careful thought to the problems of screen characterisation, and not long afterwards she opened up about these to David Barker of *Photoplay*. The interview provided an interesting insight into the core of her art.

109

'Actually, I don't get analytical about a character,' she said, 'I'm not as particular as that. I find I have to get the feeling of the character first and that feeling will then develop into something on its own.

'There's a different approach to each different phase of each character and one's performance in relation to it. What I have to do after reading the script is try to understand what she is going through and try to relate those experiences to things I have seen myself or have felt at some time.

'Arriving at the ultimate characterisation is a rather intangible thing as far as I'm concerned. A lot of people break down a script into quite minute detail. I don't. I read it once and then think about it, and think about it again and again. Going about my everyday affairs will keep it going through my mind. But it doesn't worry me or keep me awake at nights.

'Later I read the script again and think some more. And so on for maybe the third, fourth or fifth time. I don't do any extensive tearing down of the character until I get into it, until I get it right on the set and see and feel what is happening with the other people involved.'

There were, however, no immediate demands for Goldie to work herself into a new part after she had finished the gruelling process of making *The Sugarland Express*. Indeed, there was time for her to take her first vacation in several years with Gus.

After the holiday, there was yet another change of pace for Goldie. She was booked into Las Vegas to star in her own one-woman show. It was a very satisfying experience to return to the city where she had once failed to make any kind of impact as a dancer – now as a star. Her song and dance spectacular played to packed houses for three weeks and earned her exhilarating reviews. 'She's solid Goldie!' cheered the *Las Vegas Visitor*.

Unhappily, though, the success of this season, as well as having been recognised as a serious actress, was but a prelude to a gloomy winter. For her next film was to prove a disaster and also coincided with the collapse of her marriage to Gus.

The Girl from Petrovka, the story of a Russian girl who falls in love with an American journalist based in Moscow, seemed somehow doomed from the very start. Indeed, it ran into its first problems long before shooting began, when the director Robert Ellis Miller spent three frustrating weeks in Moscow in January 1973 trying to get permission to film some scenes there.

'After that trip I wouldn't even attempt to try to convince them to let me make the picture in Russia,' he said wearily to *Variety* on his return to Hollywood on January 31. 'I mean, put the political attitude of the piece aside, but the details of getting it all together would drive you up the wall. Nobody's willing to make a decision in a totalitarian set-up. It's much safer to pass on the question to a higher level – which would obviously slow down the filming schedule.'

Miller said that even if the script *were* accepted politically, he felt the minutiae would ultimately defeat the project. For example he cited the part of the script which called for the American journalist to meet a pretty girl wearing too much make-up – '*Nyet*, we do not have girls who wear too much make-up!' he was told. And when the script wanted to show people walking because they had no car, or buildings with paint peeling from the sides, Miller felt these would be vetoed 'because this is an image the government doesn't want to be seen.'

During the course of his visit – Miller also told *Variety* – he was prevented from seeing certain areas of the city, and even had some film from his camera confiscated after he had taken some harmless shots of street scenes and people.

As a result, Miller decided to switch his location shooting to Belgrade in Yugoslavia, beginning in April. Three months later these plans, too, had to be delayed, and a new starting date of September was set. Then on September 25 with the cameras ready to roll, the Yugoslavian authorities suddenly withdrew their permission.

Scriptwriter Alan Scott, who had also shared the frustrations in Moscow with Robert Miller, was on hand to explain what happened *this* time.

'We had chosen Belgrade as the city which looked most like Moscow,' he said, 'and everything had been arranged for the film there including the use of studios. But when the script was translated into Yugoslavian, we were asked to make changes, and then were told the studios were no longer available.

'*The Girl from Petrovka* is not a political film but it does mention things like shortages of consumer goods and the need for people in Moscow to have their papers in order. I can only think the sudden decision is something to do with the fact that Kosygin, the Russian premier, is visiting Belgrade at present and the Yugoslavs did not want any upsets with the Russians.'

Alan Scott's belief was, in fact, quite correct. The Communist Party newspaper in Belgrade had launched a virulent attack on the film saying that it shouldn't be made while Premier Kosygin was in the city. 'This film presents a black picture of Soviet life,' the paper thundered, 'and profanes the sacred October Revolution.'

So Robert Miller had to switch his location yet again. And

Overleaf: Goldie on location in Vienna making *Girl from Petrovka* with director Robert Ellis Miller *(left)* and co-star, Hal Holbrook.

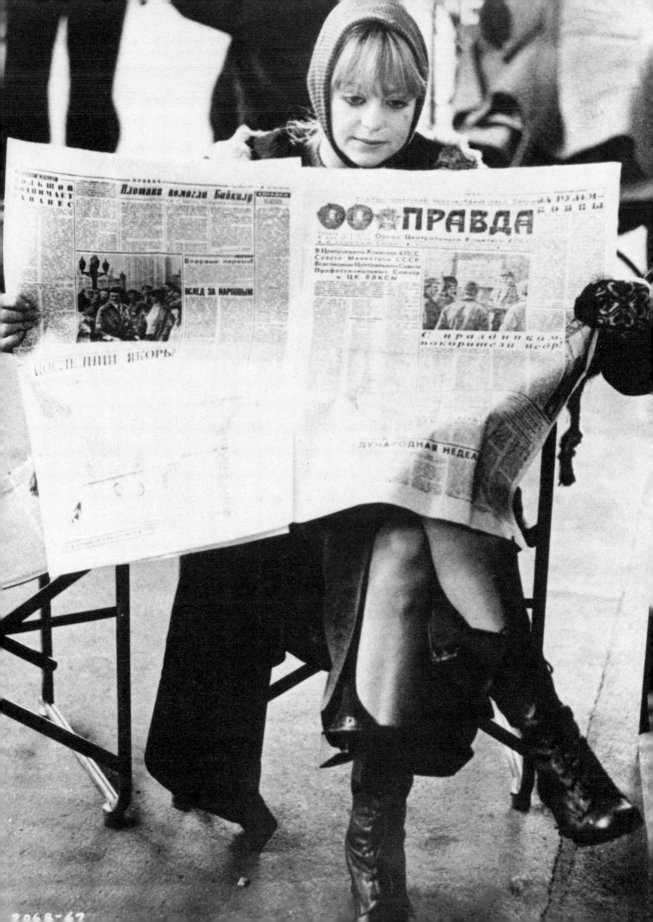

with over $300,000 already expended and not a single frame in the can, he took no chances on a third centre: opting for the 'safe' base of Vienna. Here work finally began on November 7 (appropriately the same day when, a thousand miles away in Moscow, the traditional Revolution Day Parade was taking place) and was completed on December 11 – much to everyone's obvious relief.

Despite the problems, Robert Miller put on a brave face to the press, telling them that one night sequence he had shot using Russian vehicles and actors in Soviet Army uniforms had so startled a Viennese couple walking by they were convinced the Russians had suddenly arrived in the city! He added, 'It has all worked perfectly for us here. Even the weather which was fabulously bad was just what we wanted!'

Goldie who starred in the picture as the Russian girl, Oktyabrina, was far from happy, however – and had become increasingly so as delay followed delay, each adding to her frustration. The shame was she had started out full of optimism.

'Two years ago I would not have dared to try to play a Russian girl,' she told Victor Davis just before Christmas 1973. 'But I've made three films since then and I've learned a great deal. I've expanded and I find I am pushing out my frontiers all the time.

'I hope I can do it, because this character Oktyabrina has a tremendous hold on me. When I was reading the script to decide whether to do it, I cried every morning.'

Those were to prove singularly appropriate words considering what followed!

Still, Goldie did go to Russia for four days to research her part. 'I found the Muskovites warm-hearted and hospitable,' she said on her return, 'and my time there was chockful of experiences.' Then she suffered the frustrations in Belgrade, and finally did the best she could in Vienna. But by this time her heart somehow wasn't in it, and in truth there was really little anyone could do to save the movie. Later she admitted, 'It was a nightmare. I had to pay $1,000 a week out of my salary to get a gaffer to head the lighting crew because money was so tight. But worst of all, I had to turn down *The Day of the Locust* because of it, and that was killing me.'

The Day of the Locust was John Schlesinger's much touted version of Nathanael West's savagely satirical novel about the underside of Hollywood life in the 1930s, then being filmed. The picture attracted a galaxy of stars including Donald Sutherland, Burgess Meredith, Geraldine Page, William Atherton (with whom, of course, Goldie had made *The Sugarland Express*) and Karen Black in the role which Goldie

Goldie made a special visit to Moscow in preparation for her role in *Girl from Petrovka*. 'I found the Muskovites warm-hearted and hospitable,'she said.

coveted. Although when it was released in 1975 it proved a disaster at the box office, Goldie would have been ideal in the Karen Black role. Certainly, as things transpired, she could have fared no worse than she did in *The Girl from Petrovka*!

Also suffering during the making of the film was George Feifer, the author of the original novel. He travelled to Vienna to watch some of the shooting and wrote a magazine report which gives a fascinating insight into all the dramas going on.

Feifer revealed in his article that the story was based on events he had actually witnessed in Moscow, and that Goldie's character had been a real girl. There were also real-life originals of the journalist played by Hal Holbrook, and an indefatigible Russian black marketeer, Kostya, played by Anthony Hopkins.

Despite the director Rober Miller's claims that the Viennese sets had looked like Moscow, Feifer found them 'slovenly and inaccurate'. He thought the characters of several of the Russians were 'totally misrepresented' and the whole script teamed with 'unintentional howlers'. One unnamed actor to whom he spoke told him bluntly, 'I didn't believe anything could be so disorganised, so *bad*. All I see is depressed faces. The only thing left is for us to improve the whole thing – otherwise it'll simply flop.'

Feifer was, though, completely charmed when he met Goldie. 'She is so startlingly the incarnation of Oktyabrina, the flighty adventuress with the sad past, that the sight of her before the camera squeezes my heart. I feel like a composer hearing his first symphony performed, and Miss Hawn's smile is as wide as the Volga when I tell her this. "You're made for the role. Anyone else would be unimaginable." "Do you *really* think so?" she replies. "I'm so relieved; it was hard to get myself to tackle it."'

Despite all his misgivings, Feifer did feel a little better after producer Richard Zanuck arrived in Vienna. Zanuck made no bones about the fact that the picture seemed jinxed and told him:

'There's never been anything like this in films. Believe me, this picture wouldn't have been made without the absolute single-minded devotion of Miller and Goldie, as well as my own. A minute's hesitation from any of us would have killed it – as so many are for problems a hundred times less serious.

'And Universal's perseverence after the Belgrade fiasco shows they're convinced of its potential. They're committed to it. So am I. Miller's done miracles. Don't you realise how lucky you are?'

The luck, it seemed, was all used up in just getting *The Girl from Petrovka* made – for the critics hated it and it flopped at the box office: just as the anonymous actor had feared.

Goldie once again escaped the harshest criticism and was complimented on her Russian accent. Arthur Cooper of *Newsweek* probably came up with the consensus opinion when he wrote, 'Goldie is as uncomfortably incongruous in a Russian ballerina's garb as Maya Plisetskaya would be frugging in the sand in an American beach-party flick.'

Universal Pictures, incidentally, went to court over the problems in Belgrade, suing Inex Films, a Yugoslavian film unit contracted to work for them on location shooting, and secured damages of $508,000. This was to be their sole consolation from what had proved a disastrous project from start to finish.

As if the fiasco of this picture was not enough for Goldie, it also coincided with her having to admit that her marriage to Gus – the marriage into which she had gone with such high hopes – was now over. They had separated after her show in Las Vegas, she said, the pressures caused by their divergent careers and the long periods spent apart being among the main contributing factors.

Goldie had tried hard to make the marriage work. Even as her career had skyrocketed she had steadfastly maintained that stardom and her immense popularity made no difference to their relationship. 'I think it is important to keep our professional and private lives apart,' she said in 1971. 'Basically, it all comes down to love. If you have it, marriage is wonderful. If you don't, you're stuck. My husband and I happen to love each other. And we'll develop more love for each other every day for the rest of our lives, because if we don't, we'll stop growing. And if we stop growing, both of us have had it.'

They were brave words, and Goldie had to be equally firm in replying to questions as to how Gus felt about the huge gap in their earnings. Such things didn't matter, she maintained, in a mature relationship. But how – an interviewer from *McCalls Magazine* persisted – could a man live with a woman who was nearly, if not already, a millionairess? 'It takes a lot of strength,' a serious-faced Goldie had replied, 'because we don't live in a void. People are always asking us about the money thing. Everybody's curious.'

Indeed they were – and all the more so when Goldie announced in December 1973 that she and Gus were living apart. She was at her frankest about what had happened when she talked to the British columnist, Ross Benson, in Hollywood.

'I married an older man whom I proceeded to fashion into a father figure,' she said. 'I was his little girl. I didn't know then about real love. But then one day the little girl grew up and that's when the fireworks started to fly. Both Gus and I had a very strong physical attraction for one another, but it wasn't enough to sustain the marriage. We discovered after a while we looked at life completely differently.

'He began to assume a more possessive attitude about my work. Did I have to do this and that, and why was it taking me so much away from the house? Hadn't he realised the struggle I had to get where I was? He was acting like a real macho.'

She went on: 'One of the major problems was, of course, my success. I was working but he wasn't. And he's Greek, you see, and it's very important to Greek men to bring home the bread and butter. Gus couldn't cope with it . . . my money, the house, all the pretty things that he couldn't afford and that I bought.'

Goldie also revealed that at one period she had even gone as far as advocating an 'open marriage' relationship to keep them together. She told Gus she could imagine marriage partners falling in love with someone else while they were still married, and the idea of a person being sexually satisfied by someone other than their mate needn't necessarily threaten a marriage. People needed to believe they were valuable to each other in ways apart from sexual satisfaction, she said.

'I would have said anything then that would have rationalised my staying in the marriage,' she confessed to Ross Benson. 'But in truth I don't believe in open marriage or in a no-fault/no-guilt, do-your-own-thing type of relationship. I *do* believe in fidelity.'

Because of the nature of her upbringing and the fact she admired the values her parents had given her, Goldie naturally wanted a family – and the fact that she and Gus had never had children undoubtedly contributed to the break-up, she said.

'One of the reasons we never had children was that Gus wasn't ready,' she added. 'And it's not fair to any baby to come into a world that doesn't want him or her. The baby doesn't ask to be born.'

Only recently has Gus Trikonis, now established as a successful director, talked about his side of the story: and in many respects it tallies with that of his ex-wife.

'It was Goldie's career that broke us up,' he said. 'Things changed so quickly once she became famous on *Laugh-In*. Within a year we'd moved from our little apartment to a house in Bel Air and Goldie was earning an absolute fortune. Besides, she was getting all the phone calls and the attention and I found that very difficult to live with. Goldie did everything she could to hold the marriage together, but no matter how hard she tried to reassure me I just couldn't see what she needed me for.'

'Two years ago I would never have dared play a Russian girl,' Goldie said at Christmas 1973. 'But I've expanded and I am pushing out my frontiers all the time.'

118

'It was a nightmare.'
Goldie's later comment on
Girl from Petrovka seems
to be reflected in this
moment from the film.
Off-screen, her marriage
had also failed.

And so the couple parted: Goldie to reassemble her life and try and get her career back on course after the disaster of *The Girl from Petrovka*; Gus to pursue his objective to be a writer and director. A souvenir of the marriage which Goldie kept was a painting by Gus showing a nude man and woman competing at a huge chess board for the prize of an enormous phallus. 'The Freudian significance of a male and female in competition to see which one would dominate is all too obvious,' an old friend of the former couple has since remarked.

There was, however, no attempt at a divorce for three years until 1975 when Goldie met Bill Hudson, who was to become her second husband. Believing that any bitterness between her and Gus had evaporated over the intervening years she simply asked for an annulment. The response she received to this request shocked her.

For Gus demanded the sum of $75,000 as a settlement – to which he was entitled under California's special community-property law governing husbands and wives. This sum represented precisely the cost of the couple's home in Bel Air.

Speaking in New York after she had heard this demand, Goldie said, 'Gus was always talking about his pride, playing the strong, solid Greek, refusing to allow me to pay for anything. But he never supported me a day in his life! Now he is demanding $75,000 to free me so I can marry again. I figure it's worth it – but what happened to his pride?'

Though she could barely conceal her anger at the cost of her divorce, Goldie paid up and the decree was made final in June 1976. In a final comment on this ill-fated marriage she said, 'Naturally, I did not feel too good about it. I believed that when you came to a parting of the ways, you should take out of a marriage exactly what you brought into it, neither more nor less. And if you're an able, strong-bodied man, capable of working, pride should dictate the settlement. But I bear no one any ill feelings. The past doesn't interest me anymore.'

Curiously, though she was anxious to put the past behind her, Goldie rehabilitated both her life and her career by way of the past. She once again began to visit the ballet and attend concerts of classical music. As ever, she avoided the pretentious, gossipy Hollywood parties and sought the company of her longest-standing friends. Then her film career was boosted with the help of one such friend from the past, Warren Beatty, who sought her out to appear in a movie he was going to star in and direct. The film's title bubbled with the effervescence that Goldie wanted to recapture – *Shampoo* – and so she agreed.

But appearances – and titles for that matter – can, of course, prove deceptive. . . .

6 The Turning-Out Years

GOLDIE HAD maintained her friendship with Warren Beatty ever since they had first met when making *The Heist*. And indeed after her separation from Gus Trikonis, when they were seen together discussing Warren's film, several of the Hollywood gossip magazines linked their names romantically. Certainly they enjoyed each other's company, dined together, and talked about their various interests, objectives and even problems – but Goldie never considered she was in love with Warren, or he with her.

'I look upon Warren as an incorrigible, unpredictable, zany older brother,' she said at one point. 'We get along well because our characters are so similar in many ways. We both tend to act according to instinct rather than prescribed plan, and we have an offbeat sense of humour about what strikes us as funny.'

Shampoo, the film in which Warren had invited her to co-star, was set in the Beverly Hills area with which Goldie was familiar, but her role as a would-be actress was both demanding and complex. As part of her deal for appearing in the picture, she was offered a seven per cent stake in it – her first financial interest in a movie and a sure sign of her now acknowledged drawing power at the box office.

'I look upon Warren as an incorrigible, unpredictable, zany, older brother,' Goldie says of Warren Beatty while filming *Shampoo* with him.

Overleaf: A reflective Goldie while working on *Shampoo* in 1975.

The story featured Warren as a flashy hairdresser catering to the coiffures and sexual frustrations of rich Beverly Hills women. Among these are Felicia (Lee Grant) one of his most voracious clients, Lorna (Carrie Fisher, the 17-year-old daughter of Eddie Fisher and Debbie Reynolds, later destined for fame in *Star Wars*), innocent but nonetheless sensual, and Jackie (Julie Christie) as perhaps his one true love. Plus Goldie, of course. All are entangled in a sexual web that George, the Casanova of the blow wave, weaves around himself to conceal the basic insecurity and aimlessness of his life. Though

123

the script, which Warren himself co-wrote with Robert Towne (author of the very successful *Chinatown*), was sharp-edged and evocative of a particular kind of life-style, Goldie was not without her misgivings.

'Making *Shampoo* was one of my toughest experiences,' she told an interviewer years later. 'You see, to start with I didn't like my role. I thought Jill was the least attractive character. She had no fire, she was a simple person. I thought she was uninteresting. Yet in the end, I have to admit that I absolutely love the film and that it is one of my proudest performances. I really discovered this character and that's why she worked. That kind of person is so hard to portray. In the end, it was my character who evolved into someone. She was the only one who had the strength to change. At the end, George didn't really get her. Everyone else is left writhing in muck. But she wasn't.'

Goldie again returned to the problem of this part the year after the picture was released when she was talking to Andy Warhol.

'What was interesting about *Shampoo*,' she said, 'was that Julie and I for some reason had a difficult time working together because we kept saying to each other – and Warren – "Hey, we're playing the wrong roles! You should have given me Julie's part and Julie should be doing my part." The reason being that Julie has a much more puritanical sense than I do.

'But Warren was right because it *did* work. But it was so hard for Julie and me. It was a very painful picture to do. It was as hard for her to get that character as it was for me.'

It was certainly not easy working with Warren as producer, either. They might be friends off stage, but before the cameras Goldie found he drove everyone very hard.

'He's a multi-talented individual,' she said, 'but he's very demanding. You learn a lot from Warren, but it can be very time-consuming. I didn't have a lot of laughs making *Shampoo*.'

Although some fun was what she had wanted at that moment in time, Goldie felt the picture to be an important one that illustrated the period (the eve of the 1968 Presidential election) very clearly, both politically and sexually. Though the locale was Beverly Hills, she felt it could be anywhere. And she believed the portrait of a man who preferred a life of excitement to one of commitment to the traditional values was relevant to the attitudes of a great many men.

'I think it is a picture that is going to get better and better over the years,' she also told Andy Warhol. 'I went back to see it recently and I saw more value in it than I had before.'

125

The critics also found it an outstanding picture – albeit somewhat controversial – and the public quickly turned it into a record-breaking, box office hit.

Views ranged from one extreme to the other. The veteran Stanley Kauffman bellowed, 'It's disgusting – fake porno of the most revolting kind'; while Pauline Kael once again hailed a Goldie hit. 'It's the most virtuoso example of sophisticated kaleidoscope farce that American moviemakers have ever come up with,' she wrote.

A balance was struck by Vincent Canby, the *New York Times* distinguished reviewer who said, 'It's only April, but *Shampoo* which opened in February remains the American film comedy of the year to date – a witty, furtively revolutionary, foul-mouthed comedy-of-manners cast in the fairly conventional frame of a story about the come-uppance of a small town Casanova.'

Britain's Alexander Walker matched this praise when the film reached London. '*Shampoo*,' he wrote 'is a marvellously original, hard-biting film, faultlessly acted by the natives of the very community it excoriates. The dialogue catches the endless snarl of the place . . . it constitutes a most ruthless and entertaining tragi-comedy of manners without morals.'

The demands of the picture and the tangle of emotions she was called upon to portray, plus the trauma of parting from Gus, left Goldie drained. She decided on setting her life straight before working again. Money was, after all, no longer a problem.

Nor was there anything to appeal to her in the permissive Hollywood life-style going on all around and trying hard to attract her. Indeed, from her vantage point, she was able to look at it very perceptively.

'What's happening here is partly due to the enormous affluence,' she remarked, 'and also the sheer scale of the opportunity to play around. I haven't got into that, but I hear all those sterile conversations about who's seducing who behind whose back.

'It's cold, unfeeling, desperate, and displays a frightening lack of emotion. They're just satisfying sexual urges – no words, no nothing. No wonder we have the highest divorce rate in the world.'

The words had a special emphasis for Goldie as she went through the messy parting from Gus. She also decided to part company with the agent who had landed her in the débâcle of *The Girl from Petrovka*.

For relief she went travelling. 'I just took off,' she says simply. 'I wasn't that anxious to get back to work and there were so many places I wanted to see. I had a wonderful time

Goldie with Julie Christie in *Shampoo*. 'For some time we kept thinking we should be playing each other's roles!'

127

learning about different cultures and people.'

Among the places Goldie visited during her lazy perambulations were Persia and Scandinavia where she spent a fascinating period living in a primitive settlement on a remote island.

All in all, it was a time of great change for Goldie Hawn. 'My turning-out year,' she later described it to a writer.

Then, right out of the blue, a new man walked into her life. Or, to put it more literally – he flew right into it.

Goldie was on a flight back to Los Angeles from New York in the Summer of 1975 when she became aware of a trio of darkly handsome men – obviously brothers – sitting across the aisle from her seat. One of the men, the eldest, smiled at her and soon they had fallen into conversation.

Goldie recalls that meeting clearly. 'We just started talking and seemed to hit it off right away. By the time we were due to land, he had asked me to have dinner with him. I thought, "All right, since we both have to eat." But that dinner was so wonderful, so warm, that before it was over my head was spinning. Maybe I wasn't in love at that point, but I was pretty sure our friendship was going *somewhere*.

At first glance, the idea of a star like Goldie meeting and falling in love with a man she met on a plane seems like something from a romantic movie rather than real life. But that is *precisely* how she met Bill Hudson – who, in fact, proved to be no ordinary man himself.

Born William Salerno in Portland, Oregon in 1950, he was the oldest of three boys of immigrant Italian parents. When Bill was five, his father deserted his mother, Eleanor, and brothers, Mark and Brett, leaving them to fend as best they could. Fortunately, relatives rallied around the little family, and although times were often hard, Bill was later to recall, 'When you grow up cared for and yelled at by an Italian family, you grow up loved.'

In their teens, the boys worked at a variety of jobs before their natural ability as singers made them decide to try their luck as a singing act. The early days of the Hudson Brothers – as they called themselves – were an endless round of small night-clubs and flea-pit theatres, but their determination and undoubted talent finally carried them into the big time.

When Goldie met Bill (who was four years her junior) on the plane from New York, the trio were returning from a successful series of concerts. Although she knew very little about the group at the time, fate had almost destined that their paths should cross. As Goldie explains:

'The funny thing is I'd only just heard Bill's name the week before when I had been staying at the Sherry Netherland Hotel in New York. I'd run into this huge group of fans wait-

'The world of Beverly Hills is cold, unfeeling, desperate and displays a frightening lack of emotion.' Goldie on the locale of *Shampoo*.

Overleaf: Goldie resting up on the set of *The Duchess and the Dirtwater Fox* — with thoughts of motherhood on her mind...

2740

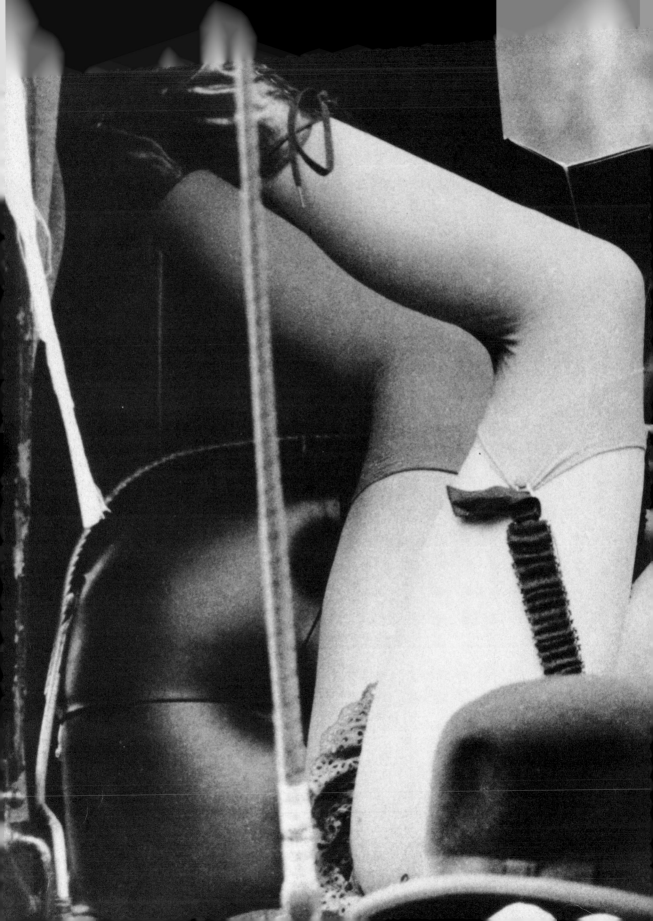

ing in the lobby for the Hudson Brothers. They looked at me as if I had seven heads when I asked, "The What Brothers?" Needless to say, I found out what a Hudson Brother is – something very special!

'It was all chance, really. If I hadn't been alone, I'd probably never have talked to that wonderful guy. Most good things happen by accident!'

Goldie could have added that if she had behaved in the way most stars do when travelling – isolating themselves from the rest of the passengers – she would not have met Bill. But her ability to retain a sense of proportion in her life, to avoid becoming self-centred and aloof, paid dividends and brought happiness back into her life after all those barren years.

Within a matter of weeks, Goldie had decided not to rush back to filming. She wanted to give her romance a chance to develop. And she was soon enthusing to the press about Bill.

'He's just the most beautiful person,' she told Roderick Mann. 'I knew from the moment I met him he wasn't the typical Hollywood manipulator. He has shown me exactly what love can be. I've just never felt this way with another man. You know something – I keep dreaming about him! Is that good?'

It clearly was. For a little over four months after their mid-air meeting, Goldie decided she wanted a child with Bill. Though not yet finally divorced from Gus, she felt the need for a baby overwhelmingly.

'I long to have a family,' she told columnist Clive Ranger in March 1976. 'I wouldn't be happy devoting the whole of my life to work, you miss too much that way. A career is interesting, but you can't invest totally in that. Just as we change and grow, other people do, and maybe there will come a day when the public won't find me as exciting as they seem to do now. But when that happens, if I've got a family it won't be the end of my life.'

But with one failed marriage behind her, Ranger asked, how did she feel about the institution of marriage as a whole.

'I believe in it,' she said emphatically. 'Marriage has lots of sides to it. There are great things about it if it's good, and lots of bad things if its bad. There were times when I was going through my separation, I guess, when I wasn't sure that I knew what marriage meant. But now I *know* what it means.'

She went on, 'Hollywood isn't the best place to have a happy marriage. Too many people pass judgements on your relationships and try to have a say in your life. It's a place where everybody's looking for love, but so few people get it. And when they see someone who has it, they're resentful. 'I'm not going to subject myself to that again, and I'm sure Bill feels the same way.'

Bill Hudson, the singer, who brought the laughter back into Goldie's life, and became her second husband in 1976.

Oveleaf: 'I wanted to do a picture full of laughs, jokes and warmth. And I also wanted to work with George Segal.' The two stars on the set of *The Duchess and the Dirtwater Fox* in 1976.

Bill, of course, knew all about how Goldie's fame had driven her and Gus apart. And since he was already a success in the music world, she reassured herself she would not be confronted by the male ego problem she faced when married to Gus.

Bill also soon came to appreciate how important family life was to Goldie – babies and all – and shared the same feelings himself.

Goldie recalled, 'Almost immediately we met, we began talking of children. Bill has an enormous capacity to love and I felt he would be a wonderful father. He seemed one of the best fathers the world had to offer.'

When Goldie announced to the press that she was pregnant the delight was there for all to see. 'Before I met Bill I felt I had given up all hope,' she told the newspapermen. 'Now I am happy. I waited because I can really appreciate this baby and everything he means to me and Bill.

'The past three years have changed my life and given me time to rethink a lot of values. It's something I've waited for for a long time. I just had to be sure the Daddy would be the right person.'

Goldie's pleasure was also shared in Hollywood. The old stigmas towards unmarried mothers had long since disappeared, and apart from being one of the city's top stars, she was also one of its most popular because of her warmth and unaffected personality. This warmth came through most noticeably when she talked of the forthcoming birth to the women's magazine *Playgirl*.

'Bill has known deep physical love and affection,' she said. 'This was important to me because I know that he's going to give that to his children, that physical love. He's going to hold them, he's going to get up in the middle of the night with them, he's not going to say, "Go away, I don't have time to talk to you right now." He's going to care about their well-being.'

Though the subject of marriage was rarely raised, that it should happen to them seemed inevitable. First, though, Goldie had to complete her separation from Gus, and there was also a new picture to make.

Right off, *The Duchess and the Dirtwater Fox* seemed a picture as full of zest and life as Goldie now felt: an absolutely ideal vehicle in which to return to the screen after her 'turning out' period.

The picture was a bawdy, comedy-Western in which Goldie played a dance hall tart with a heart of gold. (A part, incidentally, which had been originally intended for Britain's Glenda

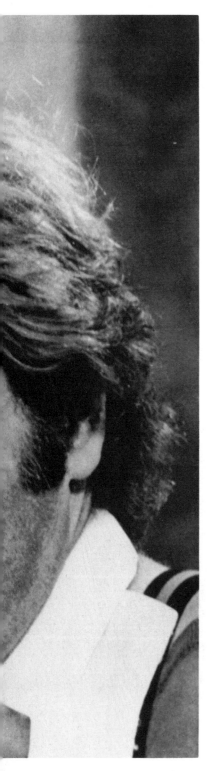

Jackson!) Co-starring with her was George Segal, an actor she had long admired.

'I decided to do *Duchess* because it was purely entertaining,' Goldie said later. 'Full of laughs, jokes and warmth. That's it's merit – it's fun to watch. I also wanted to do a picture with George Segal. It was important for my career, and also important for people to know that this type of movie was still alive. There are some terribly depressing films around, and I think those who have the gift to make people laugh should do so.'

There was also the added attraction for Goldie of working with one of Hollywood's most revered film-makers, Melvin Frank (*White Christmas*, *A Touch of Class* and the Bing Crosby and Bob Hope 'Road' films) who was not only producer and director of the movie, but had co-written it, too.

Goldie and George Segal as the accident-prone gambler, Charlie Malloy, known as 'The Dirtwater Fox', certainly proved they could make people laugh. 'I think that George and I made a great comic combination,' she commented afterwards. 'And there was a lot of fun in being a singer and dancer – it was right back where I had started out.'

In the story of the film, shot on location in Colorado, Goldie played Amanda Quaid, 'The Bluebird of Billingsgate', who becomes hitched up to Segal while he is on the run from yet another card school he has tried to defraud. Their 'partnership' moves from mutual distaste to blossoming love as they alternately dodge the clutches of a lecherous Mormon and the relentless pursuit of some angry bank robbers whose loot Malloy has purloined along the way. Its mixture of a Wild West love story, with some of the comic elements that had made *Butch Cassidy and the Sundance Kid* so popular, was not missed by the critics.

Gary Arnold of the *Washington Post* found reminders of another classic Western too. 'At the start, there's a pip of a Marlene Dietrich joke,' he wrote in his review. 'Hawn and a Barbary Coast chorus line do their bumps and grinds while singing in – get this – German! Then Hawn gets into a catfight – shades of Dietrich in *Destry Rides Again* – and the rascally director, Melvin Frank, freezes the image of her behind while she's struggling with another floozie on the bar room floor. So we read the opening credits superimposed over Goldie Hawn's anatomy!'

Britain's Margaret Hinxman of the *Daily Mail* called the picture 'a wild, wacky and perfectly timed comedy,' adding of Goldie: 'She is such a strong, self-assured comedy actress that she can wipe the floor with any opposition around.' One sequence from the film, she said, should be kept for posterity: 'The gobbledy-gook dialogue between Goldie and Segal in a

stagecoach aimed at disarming the other blandly smiling traveller.' (Goldie herself loved this particular moment. 'It was a classic,' she says, 'we were practically talking pig-Latin. The rest of the time I seemed to be riding on the back of a horse and having the living daylights scared out of me!')

Ian Christie of the *Daily Express* fell even more under Goldie's spell. 'There are more sexy ladies in the film business than you can shake a stick at,' he wrote, 'and a few funny ones. There aren't many damsels around the studio who are both sexy and funny – apart from Goldie Hawn, that is. With her bright eager smile and dishevelled blonde hair that makes her look like a wind-blown dandelion, Goldie is a genuinely original comic figure and a delightfully attractive person.'

Donald Zec of the *Daily Mirror* thought the film was 'as bawdy as a dirty postcard but much funnier, with Miss Hawn sending up every beer-slopped broad who ever plied for hire in a Western saloon.' He also believed that Goldie was now the 'Chosen One' in Hollywood.

'In a machismo dominated industry,' he wrote, 'with Streisand and Fonda flirting with politics and Elizabeth Taylor busy recasting her soulmates, Miss Hawn has cartwheeled to the top. The universal view here is that she is probably the greatest film comedienne since Judy Holliday.'

The accolades were certainly heady ones – even if the image of Goldie cartwheeling was a little inappropriate. For such an idea was certainly not in her mind by the end of making the film with her pregnancy daily becoming more evident! Equally evident was her obvious excitement at becoming a mother.

Then on July 3, 1976, just three months before the baby was due, Goldie and Bill decided to be married at the Hawn family home in Takoma Park. Whereas on the previous occasion, she had married quietly, this time she opted for a full-scale wedding, being given away by her father. Her sister Patty was bridesmaid and all the relatives and friends gathered around. Because Goldie is Jewish and Bill was a Catholic, a rabbi and a priest jointly conducted the ceremony.

Goldie had barely time to get used to being married again, however, or even getting properly settled into the couple's new home in Malibu, before the baby arrived. But the birth was not without considerable drama.

During her pregnancy, Goldie's weight shot up from 120 pounds to 170 which threw an enormous strain on her slim, five foot six inch body. Then she went a month past her time. There were obviously going to be complications, as a close friend later revealed. 'It was a very difficult birth,' the woman said. 'Everyone was frightened about Goldie's chance of survival as well as the baby's.'

Previous page: The classic sequence from *The Duchess and the Dirtwater Fox* in which Goldie and George Segal use 'pig-Latin' to disarm their fellow stagecoach passenger!

'The Bluebird of Billingsgate' – Goldie as comedienne *par excellence* in *The Duchess and the Dirtwater Fox.*

139

To facilitate the birth, Goldie underwent a painful two-hour Caesarean section in a Los Angeles hospital. Then, thankfully, she was safely delivered of an eleven-pound baby boy. She and Bill decided to call him Oliver Rutledge Hudson – a nice acknowledgement to her father's distinguished forebear.

The baby was so big that Goldie's first impression on seeing him was that he looked like a three months old infant! But she also said, 'When I first saw Oliver he was so beautiful that what I went through was worth it all.'

But the drama was not yet over. Shortly after the birth, the doctors diagnosed that the baby had developed pneumonia, and he was immediately rushed into intensive care and put on a respirator. His chances of survival were not rated highly, and all Goldie's delight evaporated into despair.

For ten days, Goldie and Bill never left the side of their sick child, praying and willing the boy to live. The heartache of those days drew the couple closer together, and proved to Goldie that Bill possessed all the instincts of love and devotion towards his child that she had suspected.

The dedicated work of the hospital staff and the vigil of the Hudsons finally paid off. Little Oliver pulled through the crisis, and was soon on the way to being given a clean bill of health.

'He had a strong will to live' was all Goldie would tell the waiting newspapermen of the drama that had occurred. She was just desperately thankful, desperately tired, and wanted to get home with her precious bundle.

It had been a close call, and as the traumatic days faded into memory, she could at last say, 'I am so happy. It was like a real storybook ending.'

There could be no doubt that Goldie considered her son a very special little boy, and that her role as a mother was the best experience of her life. She giggled that famous giggle over his cot and said, 'I'm not exaggerating when I tell my son is a genius! He's like a light bulb. When he smiles the whole room lights up.' And with another giggle she added, 'He got it all from his mother!'

The Hudsons' decision to buy a home outside the environment of Hollywood had been a deliberate one. 'This town can be a crazy one for kids whose parents are famous,' Goldie told columnist Rona Barrett. 'We want to keep Oliver away from that so he can grow up as normally as possible with a bicycle and rollerskates and that kind of thing.'

Her dream of family life was completed by Bill's wholehearted commitment to the role of being a father. 'He's fabulous,' she also told Rona Barrett. 'He gets up in the night, changes Oliver's diapers, the works. I couldn't design a better father!'

Goldie had already decided she would not work again for at least a year, and the months passed happily as Oliver grew stronger and healthier. She and Bill spent their time quietly at home avoiding the Hollywood social whirl. Goldie took an increasing interest in Bill's music – attended some of his concerts – and he for his part worked on enlarging her musical education as well as writing some songs especially for her.

Everything in Goldie's life by the autumn of 1977 seemed to be idyllic. And with the security of a man she loved and a child she adored to sustain her, she decided to take up the reins of her career once more.

All the tribulations that life could bring now *seemed* to be behind her. . . .

7 From Private to Superstar

BECAUSE THE periods of separation had been a contributing factor in the break-up of Goldie's marriage to Gus, she vowed to avoid the same pitfall when she returned to filming in October 1977. She and Bill would select their respective film and concert work with particular care so that they need never be long apart. Indeed, she had already put this resolve to the test earlier in the year when she turned down a chance to appear in the block-buster movie, *Superman*, because it would have meant several weeks of work in Britain, 5,000 miles away from home.

Instead she opted for the sardonic comedy of *Foul Play* which entailed a journey of just 400 miles up the California coast to San Francisco. Bill and baby Oliver went along with her.

Goldie was excited about making *Foul Play* for she had known about the script written by Colin Higgins for several years. In fact, she had even made an attempt to buy the rights to the story so that she could produce the movie herself. The desire to be her own woman in the film business was quite obviously growing stronger all the time, and though she was frustrated on this occasion, she was still happy to sign up to star in the movie. (The major rights in the picture were, in fact, retained by Colin Higgins – who, as a result of the sensational success of his script for the hugely-successful film, *Silver Streak*, released in 1977, decided to direct *Foul Play* himself.)

The rest of the cast were a most impressive group, lead by Chevy Chase the new sensation of American television, whose programme *Saturday Night Live* had one of the highest viewing figures in the nation. Goldie and Chevy took an immediate shine to each other.

'I think he's great,' Goldie said not long after they had

Already looking the glamorous super-star: Goldie photographed in 1977.

Overleaf: Goldie in a perilous moment during the film *Foul Play*: this was only one of several such incidents.

143

begun work. 'We're a good combination. But there's one funny thing. I seem to do a lot of working with first-timers – first-time directors, first-time actors, first-time writers. Everyone has to fulfill their destiny and I have been lucky with them all!'

And Chevy Chase also observed of his partner, 'Goldie, in her own wonderful way, has got it all covered. She is a natural and a fine actress. She is by no means a scatterbrained dingbat!'

Also appearing in *Foul Play* were Burgess Meredith, Marilyn Sokol and two of Britain's most talented entertainers, Rachel Roberts and Dudley Moore. The songs were provided by the Bee-Gees ('Stayin' Alive') and the new superstar of middle-of-the-road music, Barry Manilow ('Copacabana'). With such talent at the disposal of the producers, Thomas L. Miller and Edward K. Milkes, two former Paramount executives now working independently, Goldie reckoned the picture could hardly fail.

Arriving in San Francisco on October 31 to start location shooting, Goldie was immediately expansive about the film and her part in it to the press.

'I'm playing a librarian who unwittingly becomes involved in an assassination plot against the Pope,' she said. 'I'm an innocent victim of circumstances and someone is trying to kill me. But I don't know *who*. Is it the albino? Or the dwarf? Or the scarfaced man? Well, someone is trying to murder me, and no one will believe me except this handsome young San Francisco police detective (Chevy Chase). Naturally, a romance develops between us in the film because this is a real movie-movie. There are thrills, and shocks and lots of laughs. But it's Chevy and the others who have the really funny things to do. I just react to them and the situations which are very strange, believe me!'

And she added after a pause, 'You see, I'm not a comedienne. I'm not naturally funny. I need to play off situations. That's why the role of Gloria feels so right to me.'

For the next three and a half weeks, Goldie and the rest of the cast, along with two film crews, shot scenes all over the city, plus making excursions to Marin County. The second unit, employing seven stunt people, wrecked twenty-three cars in filming the explosive chase which climaxed the picture. Six days were also spent filming in the famed War Memorial Opera House in San Francisco.

Though she was a wife and mother, Goldie refused stand-ins for her stunt scenes. In one sequence she demonstrated her skill as a driver by taking part in a hair-raising chase up and down the roller-coaster like streets of San Francisco at speeds

All tied-up in knots: Goldie with her co-star, Chevy Chase, in *Foul Play* (1978).

146

often in excess of seventy miles an hour. In another, she had to perch on a suspended catwalk which was spinning out of control over fifty feet in the air!

Curiously enough, though, the most dangerous moment occurred when Goldie was shooting a romantic indoor scene with Chevy Chase before a smouldering fire. Suddenly, an ember shot out from the fireplace, setting Chevy's dressing-gown on fire. 'Can you imagine,' Goldie joked afterwards about this unscripted drama, 'after all those hairy car stunts nearly coming to grief while making love!'

Once the location work was completed, the cast and crew returned to Paramount Pictures Studios in Los Angeles where the rest of the shooting continued over the Christmas period until the end of January.

All the hard work and enthusiasm for *Foul Play* was more than justified when the critics later got to see the finished result. There were comparisons made by some writers to the films of Alfred Hitchcock, as well as praise for the teaming of Goldie and Chevy Chase – a partnership thought to be every bit as compelling and witty as her work with Peter Sellers.

The review of Felix Barker of the London *Evening News* was typical of several. Under the headline, 'The Enjoyable Perils of Goldie' he wrote:

'Hitchcock has done it all before, but it is still an unbeatable formula for suspense. A Little Miss Innocent unwittingly becomes involved in a series of murders, but every time she calls the police, the corpse has disappeared before they arrive.

'*Foul Play* is an excellent comedy thriller with Goldie chased, imprisoned, rendered unconscious and generally undergoing more Perils than Pauline. She has matured now, toned down that squeaky voice and more or less banished her tremulous pout. Her flimsy dresses seem most tenuously attached to her slim figure and, in Thurber's phrase, she is the kind of girl whom all men want to implore, "Put your two tiny hands in my great big ones."'

The *Observer*'s Philip French also drew more exact parallels with the work of Hitchcock.

'In *Foul Play*, his first movie as director, the screenwriter Colin Higgins has reworked Hitchcock's *The Man Who Knew Too Much* as a comedy thriller set in a highly anxious San Francisco,' he said. 'The delightful Goldie Hawn, in outsize glasses that make her look like an lovely Disney goldfish, rejoices in the name Gloria Mundy and she's given as splendidly bizarre a gang of pursuers as Audrey Hepburn was in Donen's Hitchcock pastiche, *Charade*, and a charming romantic foil in the person of Chevy Chase. . . . The film is inventive, funny and quite scary.'

Drama in *Foul Play* 1: Goldie doing her own stunt work in a car chase sequence.

Overleaf: 'I play an innocent victim of circumstances and someone is trying to kill me!' Goldie on her role in *Foul Play*.

The *Sun*'s Margaret Forman summed her colleagues up very nicely: 'The whole thing adds up to one of the funniest spoof thrillers for some time.'

There was certainly considerable satisfaction for Goldie in such reviews after an absence from the screen of almost two years – though it would be wrong to think this absence was only due to her marriage and baby. As she told an interviewer there were also a lack of *meaningful* parts for her to choose from.

'When I started, good roles for women were really hard to come by,' she said in January 1978, 'so I had to fight for every decent one I did. Now it's a little easier, but despite *Cactus Flower, Shampoo* and *The Sugarland Express*, I keep having to prove over and over I'm no longer that cute little go-go dancer in a bikini and body paint. It's a chore sometimes, but what are you going to do?

'I'm proud of much of what I've done,' she went on, 'and I think my gift is terrific, and if audiences like it, that's what I want to give them. It's a giving business we're in – at least it ought to be. But still it can be tiring.'

'I've given Goldie Hawn and her world a lot of thought. I wasn't always as secure as I am now. I had to get very introspective, to find out how to keep my feet on the ground. You

149

get to be a star, and suddenly you're a commodity. I've tried to keep myself from becoming that. Commodities don't grow, people do.'

Continuing her self-examination, Goldie added, 'Also when you get to be a star, you almost believe you don't deserve it all, and the guilt starts. Well, I discovered that's just another name for a big lack of self-respect. Because if you work hard, which I do, you *do* deserve some of the good things.

'Sometimes you give and give, and the public just takes and takes. They can be very fickle, too. You get to feeling utterly drained, and you become selfish. You're terrified of giving any more because you're afraid you haven't got it to give. But if you know yourself, respect yourself, you can keep giving freely, and so on. You replenish yourself.'

The box office success which *Foul Play* enjoyed – taking over $50 million – not surprisingly led to another picture for Goldie with Chevy Chase, but also enhanced her reputation to such a degree that her dream of becoming a producer took a step very much closer to being realised. . . .

Before all this happened, however, Goldie was off to Europe to film another picture. And with Bill having a television series to make in London, their plan never to be separated for any considerable time held good.

The new picture, an American–Italian co-production, *Viaggio Con Anita* – released as *Travels With Anita* – offered Goldie an almost wholly dramatic, strongly sexual role opposite one of Italy's leading actors, Giancarlo Giannini. With filming taking place in Rome, Goldie and Bill spent alternate weekends in the Italian capital or London.

The story, directed by Mario Monicelli, tells of a 40-year-old married man, Guido (Giancarlo Giannini) who is on his way back home to be at the bedside of his dying father. He is accompanied on his drive by Anita (Goldie), an American friend of his former mistress. She is young, beautiful, extremely sexy and very liberated in her attitudes and morals.

During the journey, Guido's car is involved in an accident and a pedestrian is seriously injured. Unable to continue the journey until the injured man recovers, the couple are drawn closer together and inevitably into a passionate relationship. Mesmerised by Anita's beauty and sexual prowess, Guido is distracted from the object of his journey. When they are able to go on, they find the old man is already dead. In the bleak finale, Guido is forced to reassess his life – and his relationship with Anita – against the sombre background of the funeral ceremony.

Though *Travels with Anita* has not been widely seen outside

Drama in *Foul Play* 2: This tranquil love-making sequence was suddenly disrupted when a smouldering ember set fire to Chevy Chase's dressing-gown!

Overleaf: Goldie co-starred with Italian heart-throb Giancarlo Giannini in the little-seen *Travels with Anita*, which she made in 1978.

152

Italy since it was released in April 1979, it was well received there – in particular by *Oggi* magazine. 'A tangle of sexual emotions reveal the contrasting morals of an older man and an emancipated young woman,' the journal's film critic wrote, 'with the delicious Goldie Hawn proving a depth of acting talent some may have believed beyond her capabilities. Her portrayal of smouldering sensuality puts many of the other so-called "Sex Symbols" to shame.'

Goldie certainly found working in Italy an interesting change from her previous work in America and Britain, as well as giving her another opportunity to demonstrate her emotional range on the screen. Those fortunate enough to have had a chance to see this largely overlooked movie will not be disappointed by its gritty realism or the strongly sensual undercurrents depicted in a way only Italian film-makers seem capable of showing.

Back home in Malibu in the late autumn of 1978, two things of major importance happened to Goldie. First, she became pregnant again. And, secondly, she was brought the idea for a film that seemed to be just what she had been looking for during her ten years in the business. The idea she felt instinctively *she* must produce.

The story was called *Private Benjamin* and it described the life of a 'poor little rich girl' named Judy Benjamin who joins the American Army with a rather misconceived idea that it will help her to sort her life out.

'There's a lot of laughs in the story,' she was to explain later. 'Not a tragedy by any means. The base of the film is very strong about a woman who doesn't know who she is, and suddenly goes through a series of experiences in a short time and comes out on the better side of it. So it's about finding yourself. And above that level, the real emphasis is on comedy, all high-action fun laced with romance.'

Goldie has also explained just how this picture, which once and for all assured her reputation as a superstar as well as proving she could be a producer too, came into her life.

'I was five months pregnant with my second child when the idea was brought to me,' she says. 'The original idea came from a girl named Nancy Meyers who was a script editor I had met a few times. Well, we seemed to hit it off. Then one day, just after she had lost her job, she brought me this outline. I loved it. I said, "You write the damned thing and I'll produce it."'

Charged-up by Goldie's enthusiasm, Nancy recruited the help of two professional screenwriters, Charles Shyer and Harvey Miller, and was soon on her way back to her with a script.

'So next I decided to form a company with the writers,' Goldie says. 'We set up a unit and launched the picture. I had to work out of my house because I was ready to give birth. I couldn't get in and out of cars too easily, so the studio heads would meet me in the living room. Now *that's* Women's Lib!'

The heavily-pregnant Goldie did not find it easy to convince these film men that her project was viable. Recalls Nancy Meyers: 'Everybody was interested in bankrolling Goldie's next picture – just so long as it wasn't *this* one. There was a general concensus that she should stick to what audiences expected of her.'

Goldie found this attitude deeply frustrating, but kept her feelings to herself. She was determined to make a deal, and would not give in.

'It wasn't easy,' she admitted later, 'and in many ways it was difficult for other people to accept the idea of my transition to producer. But I had to do it. Because there are so few films written for women, and written well, I decided I'd have to do it myself. No one was going to do it for me.

'I also had a feeling it should be done by a woman. Oh, I'm sure *someone* would have done it in the end – but probably a man and probably someone who would have gone for the jokes and left out the strong underbelly of the story. I felt *I* could preserve both.'

Her single-mindedness of purpose finally paid off when she struck a deal with Warner Brothers to finance and distribute the picture for $10 million. As her part of the arrangement she was given a fifteen per cent share of the gross income – a move which was ultimately to make her a *multi*-millionairess. But such a vision was far from her thoughts as she went about turning the idea into reality.

'You have to understand,' she was to tell *Photoplay* magazine a year later, 'what it's like to be a blonde kewpie doll in this business. When Nancy Meyers and I sat in on production meetings, the people at the table would always look at the man who was with us before answering. I'm not a big feminist, either. I was conditioned to being a female object. The hardest thing for me has been learning to act like a man. I don't think I like it!

'But the answer to all the hard work in the long run in Hollywood is success. If a movie makes money, they don't care who you are. The film industry is still a man's business, but it's getting better. Everyone has to earn their credibility, whether male or female.'

In fact, Goldie recruited a number of women to work on the production side – although to direct the picture she chose a man, the vastly experienced Howard Zieff. She was, though,

Previous page: A passionate love-making scene from *Travels with Anita*, which helped reveal 'a depth of acting talent some people may have believed beyond Goldie Hawn's capabilities', according to one critic.

Goldie put everything into *Private Benjamin* from the moment the idea was brought to her in 1978 to the completion and release of the picture in 1980.

Overleaf: Goldie with another of her screen lovers, Armand Assante, in *Private Benjamin*.

158

later to have a twinge of conscience about this appointment.

Talking to the press when Zieff was chosen, Goldie said, 'I think it's nice to have a man's point of view. And Howard has many qualities. He understands women and he's very open and has wonderful suggestions. He also has a marvellous sense of humour.

'Also, I wouldn't really consider this to be a woman's film. It doesn't hit hard on that area. It's really a film about a social strata and what goes on within.'

After *Private Benjamin* was completed, however, Goldie did admit her misgivings. 'It's unfortunate that there aren't many women directors around,' she said. 'They're so few and far between. And maybe it's because there are people like me around. Maybe I'm to blame as well. I've thought about it a lot.

'Why didn't I have a woman to direct? Well, the fact is you're taking a chance. You're taking a chance with a woman who hasn't directed before. In the end the question has to be who is the best person for the job and not who is the best woman for it. It would be foolish to narrow it down.'

But before any actual filming could begin, Goldie had to attend to the very feminine business of giving birth to her second child.

After all the drama that had surrounded Oliver's birth, Goldie approached the time of her second confinement with some trepidation. And one can understand why.

For not only had she the worries of the gamble she was about to take with her career – producing *Private Benjamin* – but she was also gambling with her very life by being a mother again. The Caesarian section which had been needed to bring Oliver into the world had put Goldie at grave risk and it required great courage to face the ordeal again. But the doughty little blonde was well up to the ordeal.

Thankfully, the baby proved smaller this time when it arrived on April 19, 1979 – a nine pound four ounce daughter delivered without problems. Goldie and Bill beamed happily and decided to call her Kate Garry Hudson. Leaving Hospital with the infant a few days later, Goldie was in raptures.

'I now have the little girl I've always wanted,' she said.

As soon as the baby was old enough to be left, Goldie threw herself back into giving birth to her other 'baby', *Private Benjamin*. It wasn't long before she found there were plenty of sceptics around, journalists in particular, who doubted whether she could made the transition from star to producer. But Goldie met them and their scepticism head on – she was going to prove she and her movie could succeed.

'I've had to earn my professional validity over the past ten years,' she said, 'by proving I can act and that my instincts are correct. Each role I've played has been a little bit different from the one before, and a little step forward.

'I wasn't happy with just being an actress and knowing my lines, sitting back and waiting for someone to create something for me. Looking back I was never completely happy with the films I did. They were always told from the man's point of view. I was there for the laughs and a little romance. What really bothered me was that I, as a woman, didn't instigate the action in a movie.'

And she added with one of those disarmingly candid smiles, 'I never had a career plan to be an actress. But I never planned to become a producer, either. The time just seemed right for becoming a business-woman. I could have gone to a big producer or a major studio and said, "I want this for my next film. Do you want to make a deal or pass?" But I really wanted to experience making my own film my own way. I've made too many films in which I did my best work, but the end result was ruined by others. This time, if it's a flop, I can safely say I ruined it myself.'

If Goldie was looking for any omens – for signs that the gods of fortune were smiling on her – she found one on the very first day of shooting. For as the cameras began to roll on the Hollywood set, President Carter was giving official consideration in Washington to the highly controversial issue of women being drafted into the Army. How timely for a film that was all about women in the services!

'That was sheer coincidence,' Goldie recalled later. 'We had no idea that would happen. How could we? But suddenly there they were talking about drafting women and of the possibilities of arming up, and here I was in fatigues every day at the studio thinking, "My God in heaven, this could really be happening!"

'It was a very heavy thought. And still is. But it *was* a coincidence. We simply loved the rather incongruous idea of this woman going into the army. The fact that the issue suddenly arose in the White House was a complete surprise.'

There were other surprises in store for Goldie, too. As when she had to be an actress one moment and the producer of the film the next. Taking directions for part of the day and then changing roles to settle a dispute with the studio bosses.

But she found it all a wonderfully exciting experience. 'It's just fabulous,' she enthused to a reporter on the set one day, 'but very tiring, too, because one is constantly having to take off one hat and put on another. And it's a difficult thing, not only for me to do, but for other people to accept.

'I mean it *is* strange for me to make the transition to pro-

Previous page: An early moment on the set of *Private Benjamin* — Goldie with her ill-fated screen husband, Albert Brooks.

The weary and bemused Private Benjamin resists the efforts of her parents, played by Sam Wanamaker and Barbara Barrie *(left)* to give up the Army.

Overleaf: Having triumphed against the odds and found herself a place in the Army, Goldie also finds love in the arms of a Frenchman (Henri Tremont) in the conclusion to *Private Benjamin*.

ducer and say one minute, "Can we get this shot before 9 am so that we do something else at 12?" and then we go back and I act and then I have to shed that and continue the "Can we try it this way please?" It's very tiring. Emotionally tiring.

'What is really beautiful about it is that it gives you an edge. It's your movie so you're able to say, "Well, I didn't see it that way. I saw it this way, let's try it." And I love that sense of freedom. Before, I'd always been cute little Goldie to everyone. But now I stand up and fight – and that's when they can call you a bitch!' she added with a grin.

Interestingly, it was Goldie's toughness that her fellow workers on *Private Benjamin* remember with especial delight. 'When we wanted someone to go head to head with the studio,' said one crew member, 'we all agreed, send in the Babe! With a smile and that irresistible vulnerability, she got what she wanted.'

Just how resolute she could be was vividly demonstrated over a very sexually explicit scene early in the picture. Even director Howard Zeiff admitted that he was worried about the sequence in which Goldie, as a young bride, is involved in oral sex with her husband on their wedding day.

But she herself had no such fears. 'They all felt it was unnecessary and would turn people off,' Goldie said later. 'But I wanted the scene because it demonstrated something about the girl's character – basically that she didn't have much self-esteem. What she valued most was having a man to take care of her. She was prepared to be a doormat.'

To those with long memories, this view represented a very substantial shift of opinion in the young woman who had been so reluctant to appear nude in *There's A Girl In My Soup*. But Goldie wanted the scene in the movie – fought for it all the way up the line – and won.

Early in 1980, with filming well on schedule, Goldie let columnist Barbra Paskin onto her set and divulged what she had learned in the interim about the business of being a producer.

'I go to see the rushes every night because I want to keep an eye on the look and feel of the picture,' she said. It's not just my performance anymore than concerns me. It's how does it look overall, how is this being lit and how are our actors doing. And that's a lot of work. Then at night I go home and I'm a mother of two children. My day doesn't end until I'm in bed, and then I collapse!'

Barbra Paskin was naturally interested to know how Goldie was coping in the world which she had earlier described as being so 'male dominated'.

'They've been okay to me really,' she said with a smile. 'I can accept the fact that I didn't come in here with ten films

The hilarious but ultimately tragic wedding sequence which opens *Private Benjamin*. Goldie with her 'husband' Albert Brooks.

under my belt as a producer, so I didn't come in like I knew everything that should happen. I asked a lot of questions. And I'll tell you this much – I've really had to earn respect. I've really had to work at it.

'But I think people are getting more used to seeing women around in key positions,' Goldie went on. 'Women are slowly attaining more validity. People like Sherry Lansing, head of Fox. Although I, on the other hand, am an actress, and of course actresses aren't supposed to have brains. Added to which I've always played a very vacant character. And I think people in showbiz are just about as easily lured as the public! So there's all of that to get through. But I think I've done it and they accept me now.'

There were difficult moments during this acceptance period, of course. Like when she had to sack a member of the film unit. 'It was right in the middle of filming,' she recalled. 'I had to fire someone for the first time in my life. It was one of the service men, because the crew weren't getting fed well enough.'

When Goldie crossed the Atlantic to complete location shooting in Paris in March 1980, she was still learning new things about the job – the money side in particular – as she revealed during a champagne reception for the press at Maxim's restaurant.

'Dollars and cents are not what I want to devote myself to,' she said, 'but I can't help learning something about it. And there are a lot of things I didn't know. For example, how and when do you approach a director? For once I'm in the position of pulling something together. I have a certain amount of control. I'm not a writer, I know that, but at least now I can get a serious hearing for my ideas.

'Yet, as producer I had to say things that would have been out of turn if I had said them as an actress. No one wanted to hear me say, "We're due in Paris on Saturday, so we must get this shot tonight. And that means we have to work until 10.30." But I took positions like that when necessary. In a few minutes they'd have the set lighted, ready to do a take. Then I'd have to strip away this executive part of me instantly and go before the cameras as the actress, malleable and compliant, to serve the needs of the scene and the director. It was an interesting thing to learn to do – to discover how to maintain the balance.'

On a more light-hearted note, though, she couldn't help adding, 'I'm terribly glad the training period is over. In the States they had me swinging from ropes and falling into mud and all sorts of things. Now I'm in Europe for something a bit easier: light duty and a little romance.'

As Goldie wound-up shooting on *Private Benjamin* not many days later, she admitted that there were parallels between her own life and that of Judy Benjamin: yet another reason why the whole project had appealed to her.

'She's pretty well had all her life cut out for her,' Goldie explained to a writer. 'She has a very strong father figure in her life and a very dear, sweet mother who does mostly what Daddy says. Judy never felt that life would be any different from the cocoon that her family has built around her.

'Her biggest goal in life really is to be the best homemaker in all of the right ways. She tries to give her husband everything he needs and not feel deprived if she's left out. This is her second marriage – her first just didn't work out. So the jolt that happens when this one breaks down puts her into a state of complete anxiety about what she'd do for the future.'

Once again, Goldie had uttered curiously prophetic words. For although *Private Benjamin* was to bring her financial security for the rest of her life and the assured status of a modern superstar, her marriage to Bill Hudson for which she had had such high hopes just a few years ago was now on the verge of collapse. . . .

8 A Free Spirit

WORK ON *Private Benjamin* did not end for Goldie when the last shot was safely in the can as it had done on all her previous movies. As the producer, there was still much to be done: including the final cut of the picture which had to be agreed with Warner Brothers.

This proved to be another traumatic period for there were arguments over several scenes about which Warners had misgivings: the oral sex incident for one. But Goldie was resolute and won most of her points – although the hassle left her with a strong determination not to be so beholden to her backers in any future movie she might produce.

'I didn't stick my neck out too much and make heavy demands,' she said later, 'because producing is a new game to me. But next time . . . then, they'd better believe me when I say something!'

But nothing could disguise the pleasure she had gained from masterminding the picture. Or from completing it almost exactly on budget: no mean feat for a first-timer. She also reckoned she had learned one of the most crucial lessons of film-making.

'I learned diplomacy,' Goldie explained. 'What many producers don't do is keep the crew happy. From all the movies I have made I know that the crew make the picture. If they're not happy, watch out!'

Nancy Meyers, who had watched from the sidelines while her basic idea grew from a dream to reality, was full of admiration for the job Goldie did. 'She put so much of herself into that picture. She gave two years of her life to it. Do you know, she even chose the advertising campaign for it? Playing against type by swapping her familiar grin for a grimace in an over-size helmet in the pouring rain!'

Before the first press screening, Goldie talked again about

the picture which was to prove a landmark in her career. 'The story is not only a big canvas for comedy,' she said, 'but it has also provided me with a chance to say some things I feel deeply about women. To show that even women from a protected background and loving parents – which I had myself – have to learn to fight for their lives. And in the film the army is the catalyst.

'I think it's got something to teach women who feel trapped. You watch the evolution of a rather depressed, very limited personality to a woman who's capable of realising her potential. I think that's a very constructive thing to show in a film, if you can show it lightly and with humour. I am very proud of *Private Benjamin*.'

And she had good reason to be. For critics everywhere loved the picture. When it opened in America just before Christmas 1980, the *New York Times* hailed it as being 'the funniest, most believable version of a liberated woman to date' while *Newsweek* in a five-page special feature called Goldie's performance 'dazzling' and predicated – accurately as it transpired – that she deserved an Oscar nomination.

That bastion of the male way of life, *Playboy*, went even more overboard than the rest. Critic Bruce Williamson wrote, 'As producer and star of *Private Benjamin*, Goldie Hawn has the dream role that reconfirms her reservation for room at the top among our finest comediennes.' And he went on:

'Among other things, *Private Benjamin* is a cunningly frivolous feminist film about a girl who doesn't start to grow up until she's pushing thirty – when she realises she's got to be her own woman, independent of her parents, husbands, the US Army and the handsome French gynaecologist lover whom she wins by writing her own GI travel orders. Barbara Barrie and Sam Wanamaker, as the soldier's overprotective mom and dad, are at least a match for Eileen Brennan and Robert Webber – both playing for horselaughs as the ballsiest Army brass. All run a close second to Goldie, and that's damned good. Efforts to resist her simply won't work – I recommend total surrender.'

When the film opened in Britain in the New Year the enthusiasm was just the same. The *Sunday Telegraph*'s David Castell declared, 'Goldie uses her honey-curled, kewpie doll sweetness like a Mata Hari of the sex war. It's a performance that has won an Oscar nomination as has that of Eileen Brennan.' The *Sun*'s Tim Ewbank also added his vote to the now common knowledge that Goldie was up for her second Oscar. 'This film,' he said, 'is lots of fun and deserves to be a smash hit.'

And a smash hit it proved to be. Within a few weeks of

A surprise for Goldie!

Overleaf: Goldie meets up with an old friend again — Chevy Chase co-stars with her in the appropriately titled *Seems Like Old Times* (1980).

opening in America *Private Benjamin* had grossed $20 million at the box office – a figure that has grown around the world to $100 million at the time of writing.

Perhaps not surprisingly, the film trade papers were soon speculating on sequels. *The Hollywood Reporter* announced in February 1981, 'The success of *Private Benjamin* has Warner Brothers eager for Goldie to continue the role. . . . There are plans to promote her through the ranks of corporal, sergeant, captain until she finally becomes President Benjamin!' An even more optimistic columnist, John Graham added: 'The men at Warners are confidently predicting that the saga will leave the phenomenally successful James Bond and Pink Panther series as also-rans!' (Goldie, in fact, has shown no inclination to play Judy Benjamin again, although Warner Brothers later developed the idea for a television series. Four half-hour shows were made with Lorna Patterson as Judy and Eileen Brennan repeating her original role as the Captain. However, the ratings were poor and the series was scrapped.)

All this acclaim was certainly heady stuff for Goldie, first-time producer and now acknowledged superstar. But behind the smile and the good humour that had pervaded much of the making of *Private Benjamin* – and when she was promoting it on both sides of the Atlantic – a private sorrow was growing. Her marriage to Bill Hudson was falling apart.

It seemed somehow cruelly appropriate that the public announcement of this fact should be made while Goldie was at work on her next picture entitled *Seems Like Old Times*, in which she was teamed with Chevy Chase for a second time.

The same elements that had driven Goldie and Gus apart had contrived once again to end the union with Bill. Despite all the effort she had put into trying to make a marriage work that for a time had been considered one of the happiest in Hollywood.

The announcement was a tersely worded statement issued in April 1980. Goldie and Bill had parted and were planning a divorce. All Goldie would add was, 'It's over – we have decided to separate.'

It was, in fact, many months before Goldie felt able to discuss what had gone wrong – and once again she was painfully honest.

Talking to John Wesley in February 1981 she said, 'I really cannot say how Bill felt about me earning the money. For God's sake, he was successful himself, but slowly it dawned on me that he resented being the second string so far as money was concerned. I didn't realise how important that is to a man.'

Although she admitted she had been working for twelve and

179

more hours a day during the production of *Private Benjamin*, she had still tried to maintain all her other roles in life.

'It was a big strain on me,' she said without a trace of self-pity, 'for I was being a mother, a wife, an actress and a producer. But I still shut off all the phones at the weekend and devoted my entire time to my family.'

But this was obviously not enough. And it was evidently her success that lay at the bottom of everything, as she further revealed to William Marshall in April 1981.

'Men can't seem to take this,' she said. 'They don't know how to handle it. I have had to kind of play down achievements because in both marriages I didn't want to be better than my man. I know what it means to a relationship, so I have always played it down. I had to pretend in both marriages that nothing was happening to me in my career. But I also wanted to enjoy my success with my husband without feeling self-centred and making him feel less of a man.

'But I have my problems, too,' she went on. 'Because I'm a movie star doesn't mean I haven't got my own hang-ups and I don't suppose I'm that easy to live with anyway.

'Believe me – money, power, success are difficult to live with or share with a man. If a woman is consumed with her work, she must find a special kind of man who won't feel rejected if she's not making him feel like king of the mountain eighty-five per cent of the time. Men must recognise that their mates have the same ambition they do.

'I'm not saying it's impossible to find a man who can take this kind of thing in a marriage – Christ, I'd jump out of the window if I thought that. My trouble is I've always been with a man who's struggling to get on in his career. So if I ever go with another man I hope it will be someone in the same success bracket as myself, my peer, you know?'

Rumours that Goldie had tried unsuccessfully to seek a reconciliation with Bill were not altogether discounted by the affectionate way she still spoke of him.

'Mr Hudson, bless his heart, is someone who gave me two beautiful children we will both always share. But his career just didn't do as well as mine. And he's a fine upstanding young American competitive man and it's hard for someone like that to live with someone established like me. We're good friends, though, and always will be,' she added.

Despite these words, Goldie could not hide her heartbreak. 'I have been through some *terrible* times in my life,' she was to say later. 'But nothing compared to that. It was the worst, the pits. My second marriage was my dream – all I *ever* wanted. I never thought that it would end, or cause me so much terror. I just never saw myself as a single woman at the age of thirty-

Previous page: Courts were in Goldie's mind in more ways than one while she was making *Seems Like Old Times*. Apart from defending her screen ex-husband (Chevy Chase), she was starting divorce proceedings against Bill Hudson.

'I have been through some *terrible* times in my life.' A poignant shot of Goldie in 1980 as her second marriage ended.

181

seven, with two children to raise, and so terribly frightened.'

Her sense of unease was not helped by the fact that – unbeknown to all but her closest friends – Goldie was receiving crank telephone calls. A man was ringing her each day threatening her life. The calls were made all the more bizarre by being accompanied by the delivery to her door of bunches of red roses! The calls became so persistent that she arranged for a 24-hour bodyguard on her home until thankfully they ceased.

It was, in truth, a bittersweet time for Goldie. The girl who had become a superstar of the movies just as badly wanted the everyday things of a good marriage, a home, children and a husband on whom she could stabilise her life. But Fate, which had dealt her enormous public acclaim on one hand, had given her private tragedy with the other.

For his part, Bill Hudson was reluctant to talk about the failure of the marriage when he filed the divorce papers on the grounds of 'irreconcilable differences'. All he would say was, 'Nothing bad is going to go on between Goldie and me. We're going to do the best for our children, including joint custody.'

Recently, though, he has been more forthcoming. 'When people said, "There they are, Goldie Hawn and her husband," it made me feel like just one of the events in her life. It invalidated what we really had with each other – our love and our relationship. I still love Goldie. Being married to her was the best thing that happened to me. I'm just beginning to understand what I've lost.'

The one thing that above all others sustained Goldie as her marriage broke up were the children, Oliver, then four, and one-year-old Kate.

'I feel insulated by their love,' she said, adding, 'I'm a mother who loves being a mother. And love for your children is quite different from love for any other person. It's the strongest thing I feel. Having children is the most important thing you do in your whole life.

'When you've got children, you have a much bigger responsibility on every level. You don't walk away from those things on the basis of an argument with your husband.'

In fact, Goldie's mother moved close to her to help her through these difficult days, and there was a nanny to take care of the children while she finished making *Seems Like Old Times*. This picture – and working once again with Chevy Chase – proved good therapy, for by the end of it she had cheered up enough to tell columnist Douglas Thompson:

'Everyone has dreams and it's not pleasant when they are shattered. But I've utilised these worries and uncertainties. I'm a woman who is no longer afraid of success.'

Marriage can turn friends into enemies — a moment from *Best Friends* (1983), which united two Hollywood super-stars, Goldie and Burt Reynolds.

And she added with a return of that infectious grin, 'Hey, I don't want to depress everybody! I've got two beautiful kids I thought I would never have. They make me happier than I've ever been in my life, and they go on making me happy.'

Seems Like Old Times had been written by that veteran of screen hits, Neil Simon, who came to the picture with seventeen films to his credit in the previous thirteen years. For once, though, he had not adhered to his usual style of basing the story on a true incident nor was it set in his native New York. The locale was the picturesque coastline of Big Sur in California. Chevy Chase played a novelist forced into robbing a bank by a gang of thugs, who then has to seek help out of his predicament from his former wife, Glenda – played by Goldie

I sympathised with Burt right from the start. We became much more than friends. I really, *really* like him.' Goldie on her co-star in *Best Friends*.

– now a successful lawyer with a soft-spot for all underdogs. (Her household, for instance, is staffed by a chauffeur who is a car thief, kitchen help who are illegal immigrants, and a gardener who is a vandal. Even her dogs are strays!)

The title for the film had been deliberately picked to relate to the madcap film comedies of the thirties, and also the lingering affection the two now-separated characters still have for each other. Explaining this, Neil Simon added, 'Farce is like juggling six balls in the air at one time. It's very difficult to keep them all going. The pace must be very fast. It's not done often because we don't have such wonderful exponents like Cary Grant and Irene Dunne any more. You need actors who are facile enough to do this kind of comedy. Luckily for me, Goldie and Chevy can do it.'

Overleaf: 'I knew her when she was a dumb blonde and she was one of the smartest people I knew even then. She is someone who makes me laugh, *really* laugh.' Burt Reynolds of his co-star in *Best Friends*.

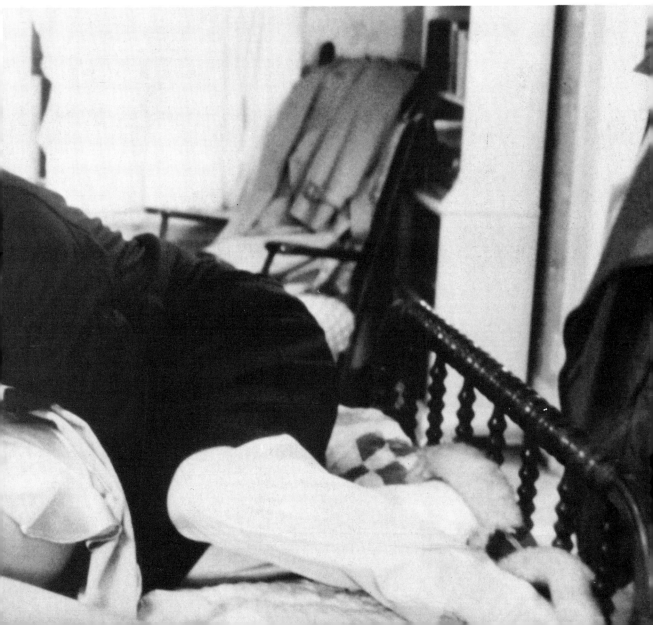

Neil Simon found his view confirmed when he worked with the two stars on the set. Of Chevy Chase he later said, 'There's a terrific quality to him. He's the bad boy in class. You never know what he's going to do. I tried to capture that in the script and also in each day's rewrites.'

Despite the problems Goldie was having in her private life, Neil was tremendously impressed by her professionalism. 'She has the two main ingredients for a film comedienne,' he said. 'She's funny and very sexy. Audiences respond on two levels to that. They are taken by it. And she's terrific to work with.'

The problems of being funny and sexy were one of the things she homed in on during a break from filming while she talked to Paul Donovan.

'As a woman, if you don't have sex appeal you don't become a big star,' she said. 'But sexuality doesn't combine too easily with comedy. Actually, that's ironic because if you have a good bedroom relationship with someone it's not until you laugh with him that it is serious.

'But people think that if you as a woman make people laugh then you lose your mystique and sexuality. Only a few women have been able to transcend that and combine both sexiness and comedy.'

When *Seems Like Old Times* was released, *Time* magazine for one thought that Goldie had joined the very select rank of actresses who could transcend these problems. 'She's the best woman comedienne since Carole Lombard,' the publication declared. The *New York Times* also thought her 'one of the brightest talents in films' and said she 'exudes sex in a manner which captivates men and yet doesn't infuriate their wives or girlfriends.'

In Britain, Arthur Thirkell of the *Daily Mirror* called the movie 'a comedy of ill-manners borrowing from the high best of Thirties cinema' with Goldie 'packing a fortissmo punch'. The reunion of Goldie and Chevy Chase also pleased the *Sunday Telegraph*'s David Castell who said, 'Goldie Hawn brings her particular fire to the role of a liberal lawyer and her teaming with Chevy Chase is once more well balanced and rewarding.'

The picture was rewarding to its backers, too, taking over $10 million in the first month of its opening in America. That same month, January, she also got some more cheering news with the announcement of her Oscar nomination.

'I'm jumping as high as a kangaroo,' she told Victor Davis while visiting London for the opening of *Private Benjamin*. 'We don't always get our just reward. I never thought I deserved that first Oscar the first time I appeared in a movie – but now I think hard work has been repaid.'

How was she coping with being single again? Davis couldn't help asking. It's not so bad,' she replied. 'There aren't enough hours in the day to do everything I want to do. You might say going to bed with an Oscar statuette isn't much fun, but at least it's peaceful!'

However, though there was obviously considerable support for Goldie in the industry (Ray Stark, the producer of *Seems Like Old Times* even placed advertisements in the Hollywood papers plugging her nomination, much to her embarrassment) she just lost out to Sissy Spacek in *Coal Miner's Daughter*. But her mood was now much more buoyant and she was pleased to have come so close to a second much-coveted award.

'If and when I do win a second Oscar,' she said to a British writer, 'it'll be so much more meaningful, and I'll appreciate it so much more. I just wish my first one had come later in my career. . . . Those once-in-a-lifetime parts just come out of the blue. And sometimes you don't really start cooking till you're older. I mean, *older*! Look at Katharine Hepburn! She didn't win a second Academy Award till she was around fifty. Not to mention the third or fourth. . . .'

The success of both these two recent pictures, had, though, assured her future – both in terms of the scripts she was offered and her bargaining power.

Goldie rightly felt she deserved a rest at this point and spent a lazy holiday alone in Africa. Refreshed by the people and places she had seen, she was in a suitably relaxed and reflective mood when she returned.

'I'm looking at two or three scripts,' she said, 'But you know, I've never chased after success in my life. I just wanted to be happy and had no great expectations. I would never trample on anyone for bigger prizes, greater success. I'm not a taker in this life. I'm a giver. I give a lot. But people who give don't necessarily get it back in terms of happiness. My pleasure comes from giving.'

She was certainly as good as her word during the rest of 1981: giving generously of her most precious commodities – her love and her time – to her two children. Indeed, she has continued ever since to place great importance on spending periods of total seclusion with Oliver and Kate.

'Motherhood is hectic, but most definitely rewarding,' she says. 'It gives you somebody – two little somebodies – to care for and consider beyond yourself, and I do believe it can make you a better person.'

Goldie also spent some time campaigning for the Democratic Party. Though not a political activist, Goldie holds strong convictions, although she prefers to stay off the subject when giving interviews.

Goldie, voted 'Best Female Star of the Year' by the National Association of Theatre Owners, is here pictured with Dudley Moore (*left*) and Steven Spielberg at the award ceremony in Miami in 1982.

'It's so Hollywood isn't it?' she says. 'Stars saying, "Oh, yes, I'll back this candidate or that one." And they don't know what they're backing half the time!'

After a peaceful Christmas with her children, Goldie felt ready to go back to work and team up with a man she had long admired. Their partnership was, in fact, instantly hailed as

Overleaf: Goldie's love for children is reflected in this delightful photograph taken a few years ago.

having 'the hottest box office potential for a decade'. The man in question was the current number one American movie idol, Burt Reynolds.

The picture was *Best Friends*, another romantic comedy – but one that set out to capture the wit, style and candour of the Thirties, while remaining free to deal with present day taboos. The possibility of Goldie and Burt making a picture together had apparently been on the cards for some time, as Burt Reynolds was quick to admit.

'Goldie and I have spent the last five years talking about doing a movie together,' he explained. 'We'd meet for dinner and compare notes on the scripts we'd read and liked, but we always ran up against the same problem. The male role always dominated the female character or vice versa. They didn't seem to be writing the kind of give-and-take comedies that Tracy and Hepburn or Cary Grant and Jean Arthur used to do.

'Then along came *Best Friends* and Goldie was as enthusiastic as I was. I told my agent to make a deal and not let money become a stumbling block. I meant it, but unfortunately he refused to take me seriously!'

Because of his immense appeal at the box office, Reynolds was in a position to ask for millions of dollars when making a picture (according to rumours, as much as five million) but always placed great emphasis on the script, as he also explained not long after work had begun on the film.

'I gravitate towards certain roles because they are what audiences expect of me,' he said, 'but every so often a script comes along which is more personal and I say, "Okay, this one's for me". It also means a great deal to work with people I enjoy. The first day on the set of *Best Friends*, for example, Goldie and I picked up each other's rhythms immediately. It was as if we had been playing the characters together for years.'

Goldie also had this feeling they were destined to make the picture together. 'I empathised with Burt right from the start,' she told a group of pressmen visiting the set. 'We became much more than friends. I haven't hit it off that good with a guy, so fast, in ages. He's not macho. He's not vain – I really, *really* like him. But please – don't print it like we're having an affair. We're not!

'Burt told me he envied me my two kids. My permanent family. You know how it goes: a woman gets a husband, lives with him, gets close to him – and the same thing applies for men, in reverse – and then is left alone, shattered for a while, wondering what happened. How we could have been so close, then be like sort of strangers? Pretending to be strangers.

'But with children, they're there forever. A huge argument,

Dancin' the night away — Goldie at a recent party in New York.

192

once they're big, that doesn't matter. If they get married, they're still friends, you can still be very close, if you both love each other. Ego isn't such an obstructive thing; they're *proud* of you! And they should be. Why can't a husband be like that? You know, husbands are a lot more fragile than little kids are.'

Both Goldie and Burt Reynolds found they could relate to the story of *Best Friends* about a couple who ultimately found they became closer and loved each other more after they had been married and divorced. Initially, when they were living together, they were 'best friends', but marriage had somehow spoiled this – and they only rediscovered true friendship after their divorce.

Much of the impact of the script was undoubtedly due to the fact that it was based on the actual experiences of its writers, Valerie Curtin and Barry Levinson. The couple who were television serial scriptwriters, had devised the idea for the film before their own marriage when they were living together. One evening, over dinner, Barry Levinson had asked Valerie, 'What is it about marriage that can turn a perfectly good relationship into a disaster area?' Her reply had been, 'I know it happens – but I can't tell you why.'

The project was, however, shelved during a period in which the rapport between the couple deepened. Then, after several years of living together, they got married and set off to meet their respective in-laws – a harrowing honeymoon that was never forgotten.

'When we returned to California,' said Barry Levinson, 'we were ready to answer our previous question – and write the script for *Best Friends*.'

Norman Jewison, who was chosen to direct the picture, felt the casting of Reynolds, 'a naturally comic inventor', and Goldie, 'a marvellous mixture of strength and vulnerability', was ideal for the small, revealing, funny little scenes with which the story abounded. He was also determined to give both his stars every chance to improvise out of their own experiences.

'I encourage improvisation only when it's relevant to the story and the actors can handle it,' he said. 'In this case it was the right approach. Burt is remarkably ingenious, and Goldie has the greatest body language of anyone I've ever known. I gave them free rein and much of what happens on the honeymoon journey between Los Angeles and Buffalo is their own invention.'

The opening scenes of the film were, in fact, shot in Buffalo in February – a plan which certain Hollywood cynics felt was courting disaster. But Norman Jewison, an experienced open-air worker on such pictures as *Fiddler on the Roof* and *Jesus Christ, Superstar* felt differently.

'Goldilocks' looking as glamorous as ever at a Los Angeles gathering of film people recently.

'We knew it would be difficult to shoot there in February,' he said later. 'But that was the whole point. We *wanted* to run into bad weather. There's a mood about being in the right place which affects everyone. Not just the actors, but the director, the cameraman, even the crew.'

Authenticity was also given by using a local house for one of the key meetings between the couple and the girl's parents. To find a suitable building, a publicity campaign had been run in the local press which asked. 'How would you like Burt Reynolds and Goldie Hawn to sleep in your bed?' The result was the discovery of a small, elegant, 80-year-old frame house on Summit Avenue in North Buffalo.

The remainder of the filming in the old David Selznick Studios in Culver City cemented the friendship of Goldie and Burt – and there was a genuine note of regret in his voice when they parted. 'There's an intelligence, openness and honesty about her, mixed with a kind of lost little girl quality which literally leaps out at you from the screen,' he said. 'I knew her when she was a dumb blonde, and she was one of the smartest people I knew even then. She's like one of Elizabeth Taylor's diamonds: there are so many facets you never know where the next sparkle is coming from. She is someone who makes me laugh, *really* laugh.'

Goldie had also enjoyed the experience. 'Now we've finally made a film together,' she said, 'all I can tell you is that making love with Burt is sheer heaven!'

There had also been the added attraction of playing a character in which once again she could see quite a lot of herself. After all she had twice seen the most blissful relationships fall apart *after* marriage. 'The film has taught me things, too. Like the people in it who realise that marriage isn't an end in itself. They really are the best of friends.'

But now that she was single again herself, did she see the kind of relationship portrayed in the picture as one that would best suit her, a columnist, George Haddad-Garcia, asked her.

'Well, I do know that living together can be fun,' she replied. 'Marriage can be *heavy* and *serious*, and sometimes a man will get all macho-like and domineering *after* the contract is signed. I got married after I was pregnant with my first child, you remember. It seemed the right thing to do. It still seems the right thing to do.'

But would Goldie live with another man in the future, rather than marry him, the writer asked. 'I can't tell you,' she said, 'But before marrying any man, I'd have to know him pretty well, know the inside of his head. And not just for me. For my children. You see we're a package deal!'

It was not long after Goldie had returned to Malibu and her

Kurt Russell in his best-known film, *Escape from New York* (1981).

196

Goldie's friend Eileen Brennan, who was seriously injured in a road accident.

children that a curious incident nearly jeopardised the release of *Best Friends*. On April 9, a messenger boy had just collected a number of cans containing the reels of film from a laboratory in New York where they were being processed. Suddenly, a man leapt from a taxi, snatched the cans from the startled boy, and ran off.

'A thief has given Norman Jewison a big headache over his new film,' the newspapers reported the following day. And although an extensive police search was carried out to recover the missing cans, no trace of them was found. Fortunately, Jewison still had the master negatives and a new set of prints was made under tight security.

The assumption of the police was that the thief wanted to make video copies of the eagerly-awaited film for sale on the black market – for there was certainly considerable interest in *Best Friends* among both fans and cinema critics. Both groups found their eager anticipation justified.

Janet Maslin of the *New York Times* called the picture 'an uproarious comedy with an element of original, offbeat comedy,' and added: 'Mr Reynolds and Miss Hawn make a surprisingly appealing team – the surprise being that two individual stellar comic actors can work so comfortably together. It frees both from their familiar images and allows them to behave in unexpected ways.' Margaret Hinxman, the doyenne of British film critics, felt much the same. 'Reynolds and Goldie Hawn catch on to the message persuasively,' she wrote. 'Neither of them has been so attractive or used their special skills so adeptly in a long time. His laid-back charm complements her pixie ebullience ideally and together with a good deal of humour they plumb the depths of that insecurity which afflicts both their professional and private lives.'

Cosmopolitan magazine made a particular point of the fact that many women would be able to identify with the problem Goldie found herself in – the fear of losing their identity in marriage and their career. 'Goldie,' the review said, 'has always represented the freedom of spirit – and here she is a bewitching mixture of strength, vulnerability and perceptive humour.'

Goldie must have found the references in the same magazine to her screen father (played by Barnard Hughes) as 'a last errant shaft of sunlight' strangely poignant. For like her real Dad, this man, too, was a person of good humour and quiet strength. And then in June 1982 Ed Hawn died.

Goldie was shattered at the loss of the man who had made her childhood such a pleasure, introduced her to the delights of music, and then set her free to make her own way in the world of entertainment. As she told David Thomas some months afterwards, 'He was very special to me. I'm not really over it yet. I don't think I'll ever be over it.'

Another personal tragedy hit Goldie that same year in October. While crossing a street in Los Angeles with her friend Eileen Brennan, they were both involved in a horrifying motor accident. A vehicle narrowly missed Goldie, but struck Eileen, breaking both her legs and fracturing her skull. Goldie was deeply shocked at what happened, and spent long hours at the hospital bedside of her friend.

From a career point of view now, Goldie was in no hurry. She knew exactly what she expected to find in a script, and until that something came along, well . . . she wouldn't be hustled.

'I look for the truth in anything I consider,' she told David Thomson. 'If it doesn't ring true, I don't care how funny it is, I don't care if the gags are so goddam funny that you drop to your knees – I cannot do it. Because I must believe the situation the woman I play is in.

'And not only do I have to believe it, I have to sympathise with it. And I have to think that it has some kind of social correlation to where we are today. These are, kind of, my parameters. I don't like to do a joke for a joke's sake. I'll rip it out if it's there for nothing. So character is very important for me. Building an honest, decent, psychologically correct character. In a word, solid.'

There was no doubt that she was 'solid' where cinemagoers were concerned. And her tremendous box office appeal was underlined in 1982 when the National Association of Theatre Owners again voted her Female Star of the Year – and she collected the award in person in Miami.

At the same time there was talk of her being teamed with two other female superstars in projects – with Barbra Streisand in a story about two friends living in New York, and with Liza Minelli in a film version of the Broadway musical, *Chicago*. So far, neither partnership has materialised.

There were rumours of new men friends, too, and although Goldie was seen out and about with the occasional fellow by her side, she made it plain that she had no plans for another permanent relationship.

Fate, though, had other ideas, and a soon-to-be special figure came into her life in February 1983, when she began work on a new film, *Swing Shift*, in Hollywood. Like *Private Benjamin*, Goldie was instrumental in setting up the picture with Warner Brothers' backing – but this time she declined to be producer. When, naturally, she was asked why, Goldie said:

'Let's put it this way – the most important thing was to

make the movie, or get somebody to make it, and I did that part. But when we found it would come in too high on the budget they were prepared to allow, I threw in my producer's fee towards the budget. In fact, everybody threw in a little something.

'The next thing that happened was Warners got investors to come in and underwrite half the picture. Anyway, they wanted the credit as producer and I was happy to give it to them. Basically, after I got the picture set up, I bowed out of it.'

'Maybe,' Goldie added with a smile, 'I will produce a picture again one day. And I'd like to direct when the children are older for that's a *totally* consuming job.'

There were some similarities between *Swing Shift* and *Private Benjamin* in that Goldie was again cast in a strong, positive role, and although she was not in uniform, the time was the Second World War and the place a Santa Monica factory making military aircraft. She played a housewife named Kay, one of the vast army of women drafted into the home front workforce.

It was the particular viewpoint of the film that had attracted Goldie, she told Barbra Paskin. 'Pictures about the war usually deal with the war *action*,' she said, 'But *Swing Shift* deals with the people at home. How they picked up the pieces of their lives, how they functioned, how they learned to live alone. It is about the women who didn't have much to do and therefore joined the work force – the way they formed companionships and danced all night and had fun!

'But it also deals with very serious things. It is not just about women, although that's the overview. You also learn about the men who didn't go to war and what they were feeling when they had to stay at home and take all the riff from the servicemen. It is certainly not a feminist picture – it shows both sides of the fence!'

Cast opposite Goldie was someone from her past – fifteen years in the past to be precise. For playing a trumpeter in a swing band with whom she falls in love was Kurt Russell, the young actor she had noticed when both had had small parts in her very first movie, *The One and Only Genuine Original Family Band* made by Walt Disney back in 1968. The tall, blonde and athletic Russell, now thirty-two, had achieved stardom himself in the intervening years, most particularly playing Elvis Presley in the 1979 movie, *Elvis*, and in the block-buster, *Escape from New York* in 1981.

Goldie found it marvellous to be meeting Kurt again. 'I mean,' she said, 'we've both been in the movies for a long time. He's been in the business even longer than me!'

Apart from being a child star, Russell had for a time been a baseball player heading for the big time. But then a shoulder injury had put an end to that career. Fortunately, as he had never completely abandoned acting – taking the occasional, out-of-season job – he was able to slip back into it again quite easily.

'And here we are together again!' Goldie beamed and gave one of those delightful giggles.

The two co-stars were soon seen entwined in each other's arms both on the set and off, and before long the gossip columns were predicting their relationship was becoming serious. 'He's the nicest person in the world,' Goldie was quoted as saying in April as filming *Swing Shift* was completed.

Had the couple thought of marriage? one journalist enquired.

'Kurt and I have talked about it,' she admitted. 'But at the moment I don't really see the point in having that piece of paper. I've been married twice and what it comes down to is dollars and cents. You always end up paying somebody a lot of money. Getting that piece of paper doesn't seem necessary to me.'

But what had quite clearly taken place was the beginning of something they both hoped would be a meaningful and caring relationship.

There was also another reunion for Goldie in her next project – a return to television in August to make a special with superstar singer Barry Manilow which dealt with a subject very close to her heart: children. Called *Goldie and Kids – Listen to Us*, the hour-long show featured her with a group of American youngsters in a series of spontaneous discussions on all sorts of topics ranging from marriage and divorce to the problems of childhood and old age. The programme, complete with musical interludes in which she sang with Manilow, was a delightful and illuminating look into her personality and beliefs.

Goldie was pleased with the show, as she later told an interviewer. 'I'm basically a very serious person,' she said, 'I've got a lot of responsibilities now, with my career and my children and I have to handle them. There is also a very serious aspect to me that has never been exploited on film. I hope I will be able to reveal that without being rejected by people who want to see me one way. What has encouraged me is the mail I got after the TV special. People said, "You're a woman now, but you haven't let us down." That was the dearest compliment they could have paid me.'

As 1983 drew to a close, friends and colleagues saw a happier and more settled Goldie than they had known for years.

She was firmly in control of the direction of her career, giving lots of attention to Oliver and Kate, and enjoying herself with Kurt and his children by an earlier marriage. However, although she had her eyes firmly set on the future and all the possibilities it held for her, the past kept obtruding in strange ways.

The *Laugh-In* programme was revived on American television (and soon thereafter in Britain) and Goldie found her children becoming committed fans. But how did she feel seeing herself again in the role that had made her famous?

'It's a very weird experience,' she told Andy Warhol in an interview in April 1984. 'In many ways, it's like looking at someone else. I don't know who that person is. It's such a strange feeling. I try to imitate that voice, the "Hi Dan and Dick and Dee-Dee-Do" to see if I can. I can't do it anymore. It's another time, another person. But there's no denying there was a kind of magic about *Laugh-In*.'

A feeling of *déjà-vu* also came over Goldie when she learned that the director of her next picture, the much-vaunted *Protocol*, was to be Herb Ross. For he was the man who had auditioned her almost twenty years earlier when she had been trying to get a part as a dancer in a Broadway musical. She hadn't got the part, but on reflection now felt it might well have been for the best. But had Herb Ross remembered their previous meeting when they got together to discuss *Protocol*?

'No,' Goldie replied as she outlined yet another twist of fate in her life. 'The thing is that his sister and my mother are very good friends. During the war – before I was born – his sister lived with my mother. So my mother and Herb knew each other. And when that Broadway musical came up and I told her about it, she said "Goldie, you call him up and tell him who you are." But I thought, heck, I'm not going to do that. If he doesn't choose me for what I've got, if I'm not right, I don't want to impose anything on him. Maybe it was lucky, because then the other things might not have happened. I could still be stuck in the chorus!'

Protocol itself also had a link with her younger days in that it was located in Washington. Perhaps more importantly, however, it dealt with a subject about which she had more than a little personal experience: that of a highly successful woman (in the film a high-ranking government protocol official) who wants to find a man who can cope with her success and also be a positive enhancement to her life. It was a dilemma, of course, she had already faced not once but twice.

The story had actually been among Goldie's projects for five years, and indeed when she was pregnant with Kate she had spent some time researching life among government circles in

Right: Apt protest by an Arab-American group while Goldie is working on her latest film, *Protocol*, in 1984 (*opposite page*).

Washington. A preliminary script had been prepared by the same team that had written *Private Benjamin* – Nancy Meyers, Charles Shyer and Harvey Miller – and then finalised by Buck Henry.

In the spring of 1984, Goldie talked about this next step in her remarkable screen career. 'I've been wanting to make it for such a long time,' she said. 'It's a movie I can see in my fantasies. Since I grew up there, I know about Washington. There's such an active social life and you can make such interesting statements that will have people falling with laughter.

'I mean, do you know what a chief of protocol does? It's one of the craziest jobs. She decides who sits where. How many doughnuts does this person rate with their coffee? I want the picture to look at women in Washington not like a soap opera, or who's going to bed with whom, but through a real story. For Washington is probably the toughest town for women, at least after Los Angeles.'

Reflecting, as it does, Goldie's own struggle in her relationships with men and her career, *Protocol* once again underlines her determination to make pictures about things to which she can relate because of her deep-seated conviction that there are millions of other women confronting the same problems, namely: is it possible to be a success in your career *and* happily married? *Can* you be a superstar and also a good mother? Clearly she thinks it *is* possible: with a lot of determination and hard work. Her philosophy of life leaves no doubt about that.

'I have to do things that I feel I believe in in life,' she said not long ago. 'I'm somebody who likes to portray people who have value, substantiality of some kind. If I believed in what the character's point of view was, that it was beneficial to your growth, to your happiness, I would portray that character. But if I felt she was leading someone down a false path I couldn't do it.

'Work that I do is carefully correlated to my own point of view. I guess those are my limitations. Maybe I am not as brave, as selfless as some people, but I cannot abandon my own sense of right and wrong. I am a highly principled person. I can't defy that in my work.'

Goldie just as obviously cares about the world as a whole and its problems, though she is not one of those public figures who rushes into print with instant solutions. She does, though, have her own ideas to offer.

'I'd say that if everyone sought an inner peace within themselves, instead of going outside themselves and seeking it in other areas which have nothing to do with their personal lives – if they could do better for themselves and achieve an inner calmness – there would be less need to express their hostilities in other directions.'

And what of her own future? 'Life's a natural progression,' she says. 'I'm sensibly working towards my own growth. I have more ideas for films – but punching in there and saying, "Now I'm going to sock 'em dead!" is definitely not my scene. I want to grow with my own life's growth. I want to be able to use it, and I think I've done it so far.'

Then she smiles that irresistible smile. 'What's past is past. I don't dwell on the negatives in life. I never have. What's important is that I still have a beautiful future to look forward to and two marvellous children to share it with.'

Goldie Hawn, the girl who came to fame on a childish giggle and a naive simplicity, has truly found her maturity and earned her world-wide fame.

Los Angeles
May 1984

Filmography

The One and Only Genuine Original Family Band
(Walt Disney Productions, 1968)
Produced by Bill Anderson; directed by Michael O'Herlihy
Story and screenplay by Lowell S. Hawley based on the book, *The Family Band* by Laura Bower Van Nuys
Starring: Walter Brennan (Grandpa Bower), Buddy Ebsen (Calvin Bower), Lesley Ann Warren (Alice Bower), John Davidson (Joe Carder), Janet Blair (Katie), Kurt Russell (Sidney), Bobby Riha (Mayo), Jon Walmsley (Quinn), Goldie Jeanne Hawn (Giggly Girl).

Cactus Flower
(Columbia Pictures, 1969)
Produced by M. J. Frankovich; directed by Gene Saks
Screenplay by I. A. L. Diamond from a stage play by Abe Burrows
Starring: Walter Matthau (Julian Winston), Ingrid Bergman (Stephanie Dickinson), Goldie Hawn (Toni Simmons), Jack Weston (Harvey Greenfield), Rick Lenz (Igor Sullivan), Vito Scotti (Senor Sanchez), Irene Hervey (Mrs Durant), Eve Bruce (Georgia), Irwin Charone (Store Manager), Matthew Saks (Nephew).

There's A Girl In My Soup
(Columbia Pictures, 1970)
Produced by M. J. Frankovich & John Boulting; directed by Roy Boulting
Screenplay by Terence Frisby based on his original play
Starring: Peter Sellers (Robert Danvers), Goldie Hawn (Marion), Tony Britton (Andrew), Nicky Henson (Jimmy), John Comer (John), Diana Dors (John's wife), Gabrielle Drake (Julia), Geraldine Sherman (Caroline), Judy Campbell (Lady Heather), Nicola Pagett (Clare), Christopher Cazenove (Nigel), Raf de la Torre (Leguestier), Thorley Walters (The Manager).

The Heist (aka **Dollars**)
(Columbia Pictures, 1971)
Produced by M. J. Frankovich; directed by Richard Brooks
Screenplay by Richard Brooks
Starring: Warren Beatty (Joe Collins), Goldie Hawn (Dawn Divine), Gert Frobe (Mr Kessel), Robert Webber (Attorney), Scott Brady (Sarge), Arthur Brauss (Candy Man), Robert Stiles (Major), Wolfgang Kieling (Granich), Robert Heron (Bodyguard), Christine Maybach (Helga), Monica Stender (Berta).

211

Butterflies Are Free
(Columbia Pictures, 1972)
Produced by M. J. Frankovich; directed by Milton Katselas
Screenplay by Leonard Gershe based upon his play
Starring: Goldie Hawn (Jill), Edward Albert (Don), Michael Glaser (Ralph), Mike Warren (Roy), Eileen Heckart (Mrs Baker).

The Sugarland Express
(Universal Pictures, 1974)
Produced by Richard D. Zanuck and David Brown; directed by Steven Spielberg
Screenplay by Steven Spielberg, Hal Barwood & Matthew Robbins
Starring: Goldie Hawn (Lou Jean), Ben Johnson (Captain Tanner), Michael Sacks (Slide), William Atherton (Clovis), Gregory Walcott (Mashburn), Steve Kanaly (Jessup), Louise Latham (Mrs Looby), Harrison Zanuck (Baby Langston), A. L. Camp (Mr Nocker), Jessie Lee Fulton (Mrs Nocker), Dean Smith (Russ Berry).

The Girl From Petrovka
(Universal Pictures, 1974)
Produced by Richard D. Zanuck and David Brown; directed by Robert Ellis Miller
Screenplay by Alan Scott and Chris Bryant, based on the novel by George Feifer
Starring: Goldie Hawn (Oktyabrina), Hal Holbrook (Joe), Anthony Hopkins (Kostya), Anton Dolin (The Ballet Master), Gregoire Alsan (Bureaucrat).

Shampoo
(Columbia Pictures, 1975)
Produced by Warren Beatty; directed by Hal Ashby
Screenplay by Robert Towne and Warren Beatty
Starring: Warren Beatty (George), Julie Christie (Jackie), Goldie Hawn (Jill), Lee Grant (Felicia), Jack Warden (Lester), Tony Bill (Johnny Pope), Carrie Fisher (Lorna), Jay Robinson (Norman), George Furth (Mr Pettis), Jaye P. Morgan (Tina), Ann Weldon (Mary), Randy Sheer (Dennis), Susanna Moore (Gloria).

The Duchess and the Dirtwater Fox
(Twentieth-Century Fox, 1976)
Produced by Melvin Frank; directed by Melvin Frank
Screenplay by Barry Sandler, Jack Rose and Melvin Frank
Starring: George Segal (Charlie Malloy), Goldie Hawn (Amanda Quaid), Conrad Janis (Gladstone), Thayer David (Widdicombe), Jennifer Lee (Trollop), Sid Gould (Rabbi), Pat Ast (Music Hall Singer), E. J. Andre (Prospector), Dick Farnsworth (Stage Coach Driver), Roy Jenson (Bloodworth), Bob Hoy (Ingersoll), Bennie Dobbins (Murphy), Walter Scott (Graves).

Travels With Anita (aka **Viaggio Con Anita**)
(United Artists Europe, 1978)
Produced by Alberto Grimaldi; directed by Mario Monicelli
Screenplay by Leo Benvenuti, Pietro De Bernardi, Tullio Pinelli and Paul Zimmerman
Starring: Giancarlo Giannini (Guido), Goldie Hawn (Anita), Claudine Auger, Aurore Clement, Renzo Montagnani, Laura Betti.

Foul Play

(Paramount, 1978)

Produced by Thomas L. Miller and Edward K. Milkis; directed by Colin Higgins

Screenplay by Colin Higgins from his own story

Starring: Goldie Hawn (Gloria Mundy), Chevy Chase (Tony Carlson), Burgess Meredith (Mr Hennesey), Rachel Roberts (Gerda Casswell), Eugene Roche (Archbishop Thorncrest), Dudley Moore (Stanley Tibbets), Marilyn Sokol (Stella), Brian Dennehy (Fergie), Marc Lawrence (Stiltskin), Don Calfa (Scarface).

Private Benjamin

(Warner Brothers, 1980)

Produced by Goldie Hawn; directed by Howard Zieff

Screenplay by Nancy Meyers, Charles Shyer and Howard Miller

Starring: Goldie Hawn (Judy Benjamin), Eileen Brennan (Captain Doreen Lewis), Armand Assante (Henri Tremont), Robert Webber (Colonel Clay Thornbush), Sam Wanamaker (Teddy Benjamin), Barbara Barrie (Harriet Benjamin), Mary Kay Place (Private Mary Lou Glass), Harry Dean Stanton (Sergeant Jim Ballard), Albert Brooks (Yale Goodman).

214

Seems Like Old Times
(Columbia Pictures, 1980)
Produced by Ray Stark; directed by Jay Sandrich
Screenplay by Neil Simon from his own story
Starring: Goldie Hawn (Glenda), Chevy Chase (Nick), Charles Grodin (Ira), Robert Guillaume (Fred), Harold Gould (Judge), George Grizzard (Governor), Yvonne Wilder (Aurora), T. K. Carter (Chester), Judd Omen (Dex), Marc Alaimo (Bee Gee), Ray Tracey (Robert), Sandy Lipton (Jean).

Best Friends
(Warner Brothers, 1983)
Produced by Norman Jewison and Patrick Palmer; directed by Norman Jewison
Screenplay by Valerie Curtin and Barry Levinson
Starring: Burt Reynolds (Richard Babson), Goldie Hawn (Paula McCullen), Jessica Tandy (Eleanor McCullen), Barnard Hughes (Tim McCullen), Audra Lindley (Ann Babson), Keenan Wynn (Tom Babson), Ron Silver (Larry Weisman), Carol Locatell (Nellie Ballou), Richard Libertini (Jorge Medina).

Swing Shift
(Warner Brothers, 1984)
Produced by Jerry Bick; directed by Jonathan Demme
Screenplay by Michael Dansicker and Sarah Schlesinger
Starring: Goldie Hawn (Kay), Kurt Russell (Tom), Christine Lahti, Belinda Carlisle, Alana Stewart.

Protocol
(Paramount Pictures, 1985)
Produced by Jerry Bick; directed by Herb Ross
Screenplay by Nancy Meyers, Charles Shyer, Howard Miller and Buck Henry
Starring: Goldie Hawn (Due to begin shooting in 1984 for release in 1985).

Acknowledgements

This book would not have been possible without the help and comments of many of Goldie's friends both in and out of show business, and I wish to record my thanks to them all here. Where they have given permission for their names to be mentioned, they are quoted in the text. I am also grateful to the following film companies for being allowed to use stills from their pictures in the book: Columbia Pictures, Universal Pictures, Twentieth Century-Fox, United Artists Corporation, Paramount Pictures and Warner Bros. Thanks also to these photographic agencies for supplying additional material: the British Film Institute, Colorific, Popperfoto and the Photo Source (Keystone, Central Press and Fox Photos).

My research was greatly helped by access to the files of various newspapers and magazines, and I should particularly like to thank: *ABC Film Review, Photoplay Monthly, TV Times, Interview, Films & Filming, Film Review, Film Dope, Film Comment, New Statesman, Films, Time, Variety, Newsweek, The Spectator, Village Voice, Rolling Stone, Esquire, New Yorker, Oggi* magazine, *Sunday* magazine, *Playboy, Daily Mail, Daily Express, Financial Times, Evening Standard, Evening News, Sunday Express, Sunday People, Daily Mirror, Sunday Telegraph, The Times, Daily Telegraph, Sunday Mirror, The Sun, Morning Star, The Guardian, New York Times, Washington Post, The Observer.*

And, lastly, my thanks go to Goldie Hawn for making the world a brighter place and for being . . . Goldie.

Peter Haining